AF271405

The Rise and Fall of the British Empire

Consequences of Decisions to Either Bless or Curse the Jewish People

(Or How to Destroy Your Empire in Two Easy Lessons)

Colonel John T. Somerville USMC (Ret.)

Copyright © 2018 John Somerville

All rights reserved. Written permission must be secured from the author to use or reproduce any part of this book.

Unless otherwise noted, all Scripture quotations are taken from THE HOLY BIBLE, NEW INTERNATIONAL VERSION®, NIV®
Copyright © 1973, 1978, 1984, 2011 by Biblica, Inc.® Used by permission. All rights reserved worldwide.

ISBN: 978-965-7542-78-1 (revised version)

Editing and Lay-out:
Petra van der Zande, Tsur Tsina Publications, Jerusalem, Israel. Editing: Linda Smith, USA

Photos, maps and illustrations:
internet, John Somerville personal collection

Contact information:
John T. Somerville
P.O. Box 664
North Fork, CA 93643, USA
Email: israel4somerville@gmail.com
Website: www.israelsomerville.com

Order information:
Email: israel4somerville@gmail.com
Or: tsurtsinapublications@gmail.com

Zion's Watchmen, a non-profit 501 (c) 3 is incorporated in Texas, committed to the biblical mandate to bless, speak out and stand with Israel and the Jewish people.

This publication was made possible by the generous contribution of Rita Adams through Casa Israel - Israel Awareness.
www. casaisrael.com

Table of Contents

Preface	4
1. Introduction	7
2. The Consequences of 'Cursing' God's Chosen people	9
3. Blessing or Cursing	12
4. How God Judges Nations	14
5. The British Empire – How it all began	17
6. The Sun Never Sets on the British Empire	35
7. A State, a Nation for the Jewish People or a National Home?	45
8. British treatment of the Land and the Jewish People	59
9. White Papers and Commissions	64
10. The Esteemed Land and People of Israel	69
11. *Exodus 1947*	72
12. Preparing for War	80
13. Missed Opportunities	90
14. The West Bank, Judea and Samaria and the "Settlements"	95
15. What Can YOU Do?	102

Information about:

a. Zion's Watchmen	108
b. Zion's Watchmen Tours	110
c. Israel Network TV	112
d. Save A Child's Heart (SACH)	113
e. Ezra International	114
f. About John and Mary Somerville	115

Selected Bibliography	116

> **"One person of integrity can make a difference."**
> **Elie Wiesel**

PREFACE

A word of 'warning': Don't look for footnotes! There aren't any.
I'm allergic to them, and this started when I wrote my Master's thesis
and Doctoral dissertation (in longhand) about a half century ago.
All that footnote silliness (before computers) was necessary to jump
through the academic hoops. So I played the game for the nit-pickin'
professors and the long-dead authors were duly noted from their dust
encrusted, long-forgotten books entombed in the stacks at The Ohio
State University.

Honestly, I don't feel I have the time nor the desire to footnote
everything that I wrote in this book. It's unfortunate that I don't
remember every little thing I read or made notecards over the past 45
years so I can give it the proper academic credit. Everything I know I
learned somewhere from somebody! There, I've said it. If I am using
some of your original material, I'm sorry about that. Just write me
and the next time I make corrections I'll be glad to give you the credit.
All the facts I wrote are believed by me to be true and the conclusions
and the stringing together of those facts are my responsibility.

In Mark 10:30 Jesus replies to Peter's statement that he and the other
Apostles had left all behind to enroll in Rabbi Yeshua's traveling
course of study. The rabbi replied to Peter's statement:

*"Listen to my words," Jesus said. "Anyone who leaves his home
behind and chooses me over children, parents, family, and
possessions, all for the sake of the gospel, it will come   back to him
a hundred times as much in this lifetime—homes, family, mothers,
brothers, sisters, children, possessions—along with persecutions.
And in the age to come, he will inherit eternal life."*

While on the road, whenever I had the opportunity, I would teach the
message of the imperative truth of Christians needing to be a blessing
to the Jews. It seem to me that seldom is this universal truth being
taught or put into practice anywhere in the world.

However, as always, God fulfills His Promises bigger than we ever imagined. As I traveled across the Central U.S. and in Israel with that message, God started providing me with homes to stay in and families who adopted my wife and me as if we were their children.

Then I began to get acquainted with my new "brothers" and "sisters" who had the same zeal and love in their hearts for the Jewish people that God had implanted in ours. I never had a sister and always wished I had one, but I did have some female cousins that I thought the world of. In fulfillment of Mark 10, in practically every city where I taught, I found a "sister" who was already the nexus or the link to other believers with the same heart for loving and helping the Jewish people.

There are two special sisters of mine whose care, patience and godly love for Mary and me I wish to honor and thank. This book and others like it would never have seen the light of day without the help, support and the gentle but firm prodding that was needed to put these teachings down on paper. These sisters literally came from the corners of the earth to meet their new brother (me) at the center of the planet in Jerusalem.

Both of them have lives and ministries that could fill at least several volumes for the lives they have blessed and continue to do so.

Rita Adams, born in Brazil, found me by way of her homes in Texas and Jerusalem. Rita is like an Israeli-powered comet that leaves a fiery trail of ideas and support for all things related to loving the Jews and Israel. This book is just one little spark from that trail she continues to blaze.

Petra van der Zande came from Holland and also is privileged to make her home in Jerusalem. Her life, like that of her "sister" Rita, is dedicated to serving the God and People of Israel.

Both of these sisters of mine have strong husbands who are perfect matches for their wives. Together, they are two godly couples whose cooperation and support for their spouses have been an ongoing inspiration to Mary and me.

There are also a couple of men who provided the brotherly push just at the right time to keep me going on this project.

Pastor Larry Ollison, who has authored numerous books (with real footnotes), pointed out to me that DVDs, CDs and tapes don't last. Someone may listen to them once and then they disappear. A book however, remains on your shelf and over the years, you may often go back to it.   As he said that to me I looked at my overflowing bookshelves and I had to agree. So I got back to writing.

Pastor David Simmons, my longtime cowboy partner and friend, is another godly-provided brother who so often (and way beyond the normal call of duty) picked up the slack in our ministry by joyfully doing the things he knows that I hate to do, so I could keep focused on this work. It should go without saying (but I am saying it in case somebody might miss it), both of these brothers of mine also have wives who are their true helpmates and integral parts of their dynamic ministries.

John Somerville
Summer 2018

CHAPTER 1
Introduction

There are universal laws that God set in motion that are unconditional. No matter the age or dispensation – they are going to work.
You can ignore them, but you can't stop them from working.
When it comes to the NATION OF ISRAEL, which was chosen by God to be a witness of Himself, in a nutshell He promised and warned in Genesis 12:3,

> **"I will bless those who bless you [Abraham and his descendants], and the one who curses you I will curse."**

Zechariah 2:8 further warns the nations of the world about their treatment of the Nation and the Land of Israel:
"He has sent me against the nations which plunder you, for he who touches you, touches the apple [pupil] of [the Lord's] eye."

These are severe warnings, especially to national leaders.

I've often wondered how many people ever think about these issues. For years, I presumed most people saw things the way I did. That changed when I started speaking before groups on issues like physical fitness, health and exercise. It was then that I began to realize that often I was on a different wavelength from those whom I addressed. After a while (I'm rather slow on the uptake), I realized that most people might agree with the premise and even the conclusions of my presentations, but they seldom put their mental assent into action. It is one thing for individuals to ignore healthy living habits. One visit to your local Walmart will graphically illustrate the need for wide aisles.

However, after becoming more interested in political issues which not only affected me, but my children and grandchildren as well, I became very concerned about our nation's spiritual direction and future.

I had no problem believing that God would judge me about how I personally lived. But then I wondered, *will God also judge or reward nations for their practices, laws and policies? Are entire nations judged by the practices of the leader they follow or have elected?*

Of the 193 nations recognized by the United Nations, only 45% are fully democratic – their citizens had a choice in the leadership they chose. **Will the way an entire nation is judged be based on the actions of its leader?**

Some theologians persuasively argue from Scripture that in this present dispensational age, God is not judging nations as He has done in the past but will do so in a future age. Even if that is correct, it still does not remove the consequences of "cursing" the Jews (Gen. 12:3) and "dividing the Land" (Joel 3:2).

These consequences continue to apply to national leaders as well as to individuals. I have come to believe that when national leaders are violating the clear message of the Word, they and their followers will suffer the consequences.

What do you think about that?

CHAPTER 2
The Consequences of 'Cursing'
God's Chosen People

What are the consequences of violating that principle of cursing the Chosen People and/or dividing the Promised Land?
The consequences are an endless variety of His choosing. Scriptures show they range from hemorrhoids to floods, fires and earthquakes and all the stops in between and beyond. When wicked leaders misdirect national policies against the Jews and/or Israel, the people they rule often suffer a fallout from the consequences.

Proverbs 29:2 is an apt summary:
>*"When the righteous are in authority, the people rejoice,*
>*But when the wicked rule, the people mourn."*

What are the consequences when national policies or laws are blatantly contrary to plain biblical directions?
Much of it has to do with its leadership.
We know from Genesis 12:3 that we are supposed to be a blessing to the Jewish people because God said to Abraham,

> *"I'm going to make you a great nation. And I'm going to bless those who bless you and the one that curses you, I'm going to curse. And in you, all the families in the earth will be blessed."*

Is God judging the United States?
Attempting to pinpoint God's judgment to a person, event, or country is a serious and precarious endeavor. However, nothing happens unless God allows it, or He causes it to occur.

In biblical times, prophets warned the people about God's coming judgment. God gave the Canaanites 400 years to repent and Nineveh 40 days to repent. He told Abraham that if He was able to find ten righteous men in Sodom and Gomorrah, He would not destroy those cities.

Studying the history on how different countries and cultures treated the Jews shows one recurrent pattern: those that treated the Jews fairly, their provinces and nations were blessed by God.

However, when the Gentile nation changed its attitude and practices toward the Jewish people, they received the recompense of their actions. Eventually, both the people and their country were cursed and consequently lost all power, money and protection from their enemies.

Even today there are unseen spiritual laws that govern man's actions, either good or bad.

> *"Do not be deceived: God cannot be mocked.*
> *A man reaps what he sows."* Galatians 6:7 NIV.

This applies to individuals, groups and governments.

> *"I will bless those who bless you,*
> *and whoever curses you I will curse"* Genesis 12:3

Examine Genesis 12: 1-3 closely. It is blatantly obvious to me that this universal promise of blessing and cursing is related to the Jews and the Land of Israel. It is not suspended during this dispensation – this universal principle is UNCONDITIONAL.

God's **unconditional** promise to all mankind is applicable to:

- Individuals
- Families, Tribes, Clans
- Churches, Synagogues
- Communities
- Nations

It doesn't matter **WHO** blesses the descendants of Abraham or the Jewish people - God **IS** going to bless them. Why? Because He has limited Himself by His Word.

Figuratively, He has tied His own hands by His promise, for He said, "I'm going to do it!"

"For thou hast magnified thy word above all thy name."

This is similar to God writing a check and signing His name under the amount on the check. That check is not the money, but it is a promise that the money is in the account and to whomever the check is written can draw on that account. The character of someone who 'bounces' checks is not good. However, God has put His promises above His name. When He puts his autograph down under His promise... His good and perfect names guarantees the promise. And you can take that to the bank! Hustle down to the nearest bank and cash it in.

Is it necessary that I repeat it again? How about this time you repeat it out loud with me? I know I'm not there, but just pretend I am. I'm sure that you trust yourself more than me. Do you trust your own voice? After all, you've been hearing it all your life. Now speak it out loud and listen to your own voice and words.

Here we go! Repeat LOUDLY after me,

"God will bless those who bless the Jews and God will curse those who curse the Jews. I know this is true because it says so in black and white in God's Word and I choose to believe it!"

Now, Whoa! Don't stop yet! I want you to ask yourself something rather formally:

Do you (insert your full name here, including that middle name you keep hiding) _____.

DO you _____ want to be blessed by God or cursed by God? Hint: Don't be an idiot... go for the blessing!

ONE MORE TIME.

"I, _____ , being of sound mind, choose to be blessed by God Almighty because I choose to bless the Jews. It is solemnly stated in Genesis 12: 1-3 and I will believe it and will practice it."

CHAPTER 3
Blessing or Cursing?

How is a nation blessed by God?

It can be done in many ways.

That nation can be given godly leaders who will administer laws and judge fairly; they are truly concerned and provide help for the poor and needy.

A nation can be blessed with previously undiscovered resources.

It can be blessed with proper amounts of water, rain, fertile soil and sunshine. It can be blessed with prosperity.

In short, all the blessings promised to the Children of Israel in Deuteronomy 28 will apply to other nations as well.

The meaning of "curse"

I will curse those who curse you... in Genesis 12 does not mean swearing or cussing but:

    a. To treat with contempt

    b. To slight someone because they are Jewish.

    c. To purposely ignore them. This can be done on a national basis. You can pull out of the Middle-East (as our former administration did) and ignore the problems.

    d. To dis-esteem something that God has esteemed.

Now this is very important to understand:

God has **esteemed** the children of Israel as His chosen nation and He has **esteemed** the Land of Israel as His personal piece of property, because He calls it "MY LAND" at least eight times in Scriptures.

It belongs to Him! All He had to do is call it "MY LAND" once, and we would know it. By saying it eight times, God emphasizes the point He is making.

Not teaching the Biblical truth about Israel is to **dis-esteem** Abraham's descendants as well as God's plan and purposes for them and for Israel. Whether or not it is done on purpose or inadvertently, it is still a curse.

Pastors! If you are still awake.... When was the last time you preached a series on "Israel and the Jews in God's Plan" or any series like that? I'll bet "never" is the honest answer.

By studying how different nations and kingdoms treated the Jews, I learned that when they invited them into their countries, especially in some of those small European countries, God blessed them abundantly.

However, by turning against the Jews, as these countries inevitably did, they lost their world standing and the blessing of God was lifted from that empire.

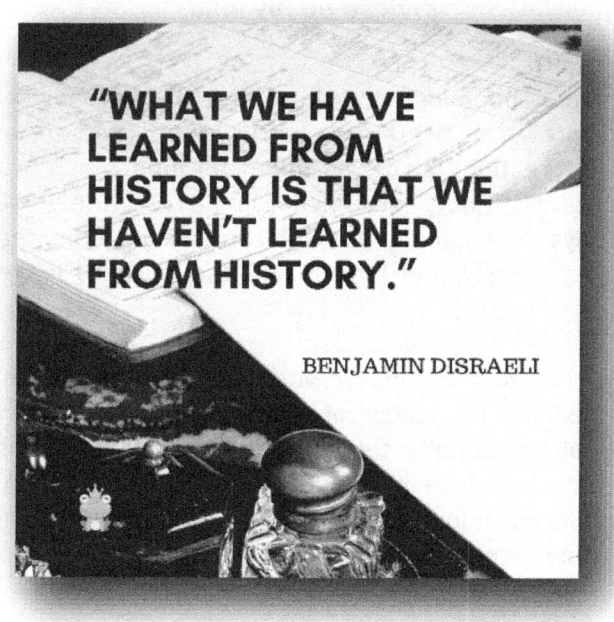

"WHAT WE HAVE LEARNED FROM HISTORY IS THAT WE HAVEN'T LEARNED FROM HISTORY."

BENJAMIN DISRAELI

CHAPTER 4
How God Judges Nations

Is God judging nations? I tried to get this question into the presidential debates because I wanted the candidates to address that question.

Is it important? How does it work? Does God really judge nations?
Joel 3:1,2 gives us the answer:

> *"In those days and at that time, when I restore the fortunes of Judah and Jerusalem, I will gather all nations and bring them down to the Valley of Jehoshaphat. There I will put them on trial for what they did to my inheritance, my people Israel, because they scattered my people among the nations and divided up my land."*

Today, Israel is booming - the prosperity, the fortunes of Judah and Jerusalem are again being restored in Israel. They are as great, or maybe even greater, than during Solomon's time.
This is happening today, not someday in the far future – TODAY!
And God says: *"I'm going to gather all nations and bring them down to the valley of Jehoshaphat* [This means the Valley of Judgement] *and there I'll judge them."*

When referring to 'nations', we often use the name of a nation while actually meaning the leader of that country. For instance, people talked about Russia being the adversary while meaning Joseph Stalin. Some of his successors - Khrushchev, Gorbachev, and Putin – were not the actual Soviet Union or Russia, but in their capacity as leaders they were the embodiment of the country.

Would a nation's entire population be judged, found guilty and punished for the sins of a leader? Even the innocent righteous people who also happen to live there?
Biblical history teaches us that God is just, merciful and patient.

"...when the wicked rule, the people groan." Proverbs 29:2

Throughout history we have seen that nations were judged, are being judged, and are going to be judged on their treatment of "My people Israel".

Joel 3 tells us that God is going to judge all nations concerning His "inheritance" and explains it by defining "Inheritance" as "My People Israel."
What does it mean that nations are going to be judged on "My people Israel"?
"For they scattered My people among the nations," – they drove them out of the land.
From history we know which nations were guilty of that.

Our next question is: **have some nations kept them scattered?**
When the Jews wanted to return, when God was calling them back, did certain nations say: "No, sorry, you can't come in here!"
Yes, they did. This publication is about the empire that did just that.

Not only will God judge nations because they scattered His people, but also because they did something that was really profound: *"**They divided up My land"**.* They divided up God's land - they cut it and chopped it up, this small, tiny land which today is only 8,000 sq. miles. It's nothing (less than 1%) in comparison to its Arab neighbor's lands.

I live in a 2,000 sq. mile county named Madera adjoined by Fresno county, together we are 8,000 sq. miles – the same size as the state of Israel today.
When I tell people where I live they exclaim, "Get out of here! It can't be! We read about Israel all the time, it's a big country, always in the papers. And we are never in the papers."

Twenty times the country of Israel fits inside the state of California and 33 times inside of Texas!

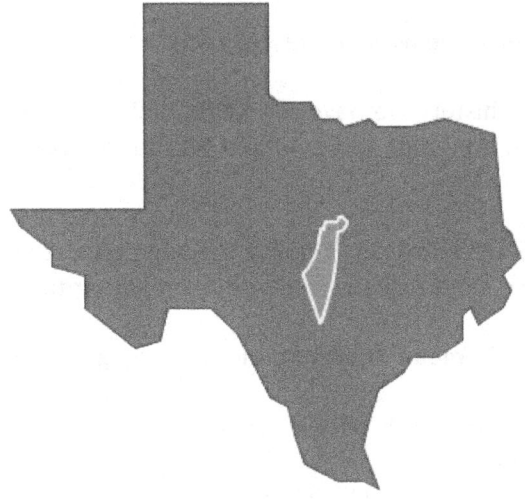

This tiny piece of property was made by God. He is the God of the universe, Who created all the lands on the earth. And He said: "I'm going to reserve one little piece of property; it is specifically mine, and it is for My People."

From Joel 3:2 we learned that God is going to judge nations on:
1. Do they scatter His people or keep them scattered, and
2. Did they ever divide up My land?

As we are now beginning the in-depth study of the British Empire, we'll learn what happened to them when they first became a blessing but ended up being a curse to the Apple of God's eye.

CHAPTER 5
The British Empire – How it All Began

The British Empire, the greatest, largest empire in the history of the world, began in the year 1200.

The British Isles were a windswept, wet island off the northwest coast of Europe.

The early rulers noticed that fleets from nearby countries such as Holland, Spain and Portugal were sailing around the world, bringing back gold and other valuable things.

Unable to dig for gold themselves, the Brits became pirates and stole the merchandize from ships sailing back to their home countries.

In 1243, the Jew-hating King Henry III granted the first privateer commission - the Letter of Reprisal or 'Marque' – which read in part, "to annoy our enemies by sea, and by land wheresoever they are able, so that they share with us one half of all their gain."

These letters licensed a ship to attack enemy ships without fear of punishment. In exchange, the king received a share of all plunder and was able to increase the size of his navy without having to pay crews, train, maintain, or supply them.

Originally, ships granted such licenses were called "private men-of-war," but this was shortened to "privateer". This actually meant a pirate ship working for and in conjunction with the English Crown.

Drake viewing treasure taken from a Spanish ship

Privateering flourished between the 16th and 18th centuries. Queen Elizabeth I's (1533 – 1603) privateers were known as Sea Dogs. The best known of these was Sir Francis Drake, whom she called "her pirate".

Thievery hardly seems the way to start a world empire, but that is how the British did it.

The slave trade and piracy became interlocked when John Hawkins, one of the English privateers, stole slaves from Portuguese traders in 1562. Not being heavily armed compared to the gold ships, they were much easier to attack and from then on, they began capturing slave ships. The entrepreneurs decided to get into the less risky black slavery business themselves and thus the pirates began hauling slaves from Africa to the new world.

Medieval England's Anti-Semitism

Jewish merchants and their families first entered England alongside William the Conqueror in 1066. He put them in a special category by declaring that they were his private subjects unlike the rest of the population. This put them in a unique but ambivalent legal position in that they were not tied to any particular lord as were other serfs, but they were subject to the whims of whoever became king.

Every successive king following William had to formally review the royal charter, granting Jews the right to remain in England. However, Jews did not enjoy any of the hard won guarantees that were in the Magna Carta of 1215.

To no man will we sell, or deny, or delay, right or justice.

The Magna Carta

Economically, Jews played a key role in the country because they were useful for usury. The Roman Church had long forbidden the lending of money for profit by Christians. However, loans were always needed, and the Church and the rulers could get their cut if they employed Jews as money lenders.

Church law did not apply to Jews and Jewish law did not forbid lending with interest to non-Jews. The Jewish profits from those loans were heavily taxed by the king. Because they were uniquely his subjects, he could levy increased taxes on them at will without having to summon Parliament.

Other forms of employment such as farming, guild membership, etc. were closed to Jews. They were type-cast as money lenders who were thinly disguised as extortioners preying upon the good but cash-strapped Christians.

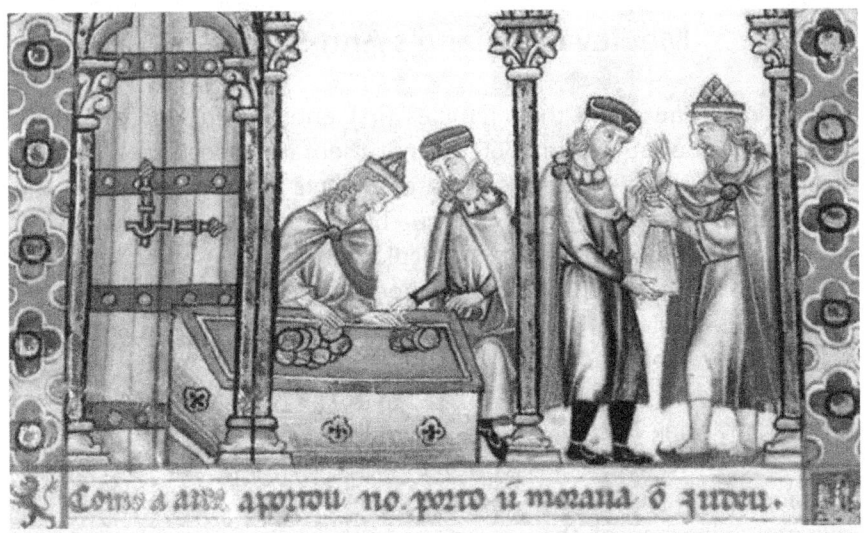

The Jewish reputation became a combination of Judas Iscariot and Shylock the Moneylender, wrapped in the cloak and curse of the perpetually wandering Christ-Killers looking for innocent Christian children to sacrifice for their Passover rituals. While an anti-Jewish attitude was widespread in Europe, medieval England was particularly anti-Jewish.

In 1239, King Henry III introduced even more stringent policies on the Jews based on his own hatred of them and also in response to the increasing pressure on Henry from the Roman papacy. Jewish leaders across England were imprisoned and forced to pay fines equivalent to a third of their goods, and any outstanding loans to non-Jews were to be released without payment. Further huge demands for more cash followed in 1244. These ever-increasing demands eventually destroyed the ability of the Jewish community to lend money commercially. The financial extortion Henry placed on the Jews caused them to force repayment of the loans they had placed, which fueled even more anti-Jewish resentment across the kingdom.

Taken together Henry's policies of excessive Jewish taxation, anti-Jewish legislation, bowing to Rome's pressure and anti-Jewish propaganda were all causes for Jewish hatred that raised an impregnable wall around the Jew. This anti-Semitic hatred had been built precept upon precept, one lie upon another lie.

By 1290, fifteen years after Henry's death and the succession of Edward I, the formal King's Edict of Expulsion was levied on all the Jews resident in England and was carried out on the Christian All-Saints Day.

This ban on Jews lasted for more than three and a half centuries. That long dark period of England being under the biblical curse of Genesis 12 was marked by an economy which grew as the result of piracy, slave trading and theft. Quite a foundation!

Another curse placed on Abraham's descendants was a thinly veiled forced conversion attempt by Henry when he built the *Domus Conversororum* (House of Converts) in London to assist those Jews who had made the commitment to Christianity. It was a communal home and offered some low wages, because all the Jews who converted to Christianity had to forfeit all their possessions.

HOME FOR CONVERTED JEWS, OR DOMUS CONVERSORUM, OXFORD.
Founded 1235; demolished 1750.

For those Jews forced into penury this was often the last resort.

It is estimated that as many as 10 percent of the Jews in England had been converted by the late 1250s, in large part due to their deteriorating economic conditions.

Britain became deeply involved in the slave trade during the 16th century. By 1783, the triangular route shipped British-made goods to Africa to buy slaves, transported the enslaved to the West Indies, and then delivered slave-grown products such as sugar, tobacco and cotton to Britain. After a short turn-around, the same ship sailed to Africa to pick up more slaves. The slave trade eventually represented about 80 percent of Great Britain's foreign income.

The route they took was named 'the Middle-passage' – a very long, tortuous and ultimately deadly passage. Over the years, they undoubtedly transported millions of people from west Africa. Agents even used African tribes to go into the interior, steal men from other tribes and bring them to the coast. The Brits put them into their ships and brought them to the Americas.

Of the estimated 11 million Africans transported to be sold into slavery, about 1.4 million died during the voyage.

This infamously tragic triangular trade route was the financial basis of the empire's growth and the building of the British Empire in the centuries to come. It is obvious that it would be very difficult to get rid of an enterprise that was so vitally important to the economy.

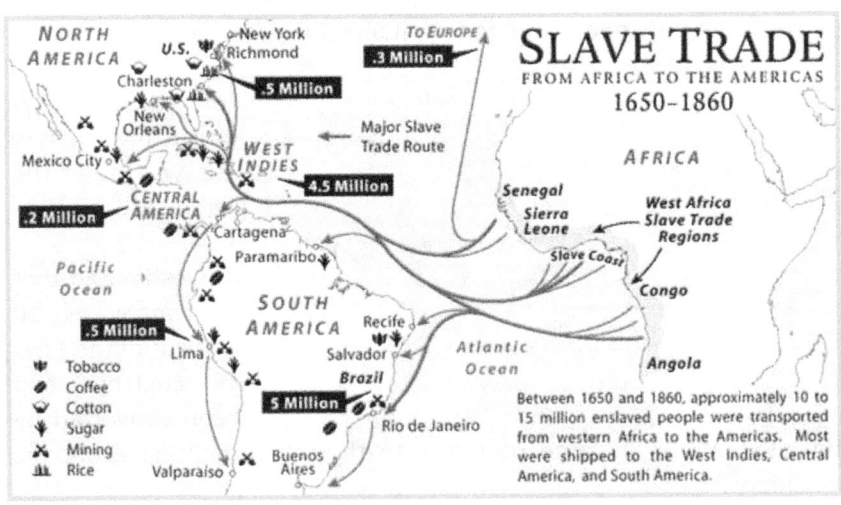

In the 13th century, King Edward I kicked out the Jews. This 'curse' was spewed out by the leader of the British Isles around the same time that the piracy was beginning to take hold.

Oliver Cromwell (1599 – 1658) was an English military and political leader who became Lord Protector of England, Scotland and Ireland. In 1656, more than 365 years since the Jewish expulsion from England, he called a conference on the question of allowing their return, reasoning that the Jews in Holland added greatly to the economic growth of Britain's rival. Even though he ran into unexpected opposition from merchants and some clergy, Cromwell prevailed by some politically-adept maneuvering. Quietly, the Jews began to return to England. Cromwell's pro-Jewish stance wasn't only because of the financial

aspects. Because of his own deeply-held religious beliefs (as well as that of many English citizens of that time), he believed that there had to be religious freedom for all, except Roman Catholics. Cromwell probably believed that the returning Jews and their eventual conversion to Christianity would hasten the return of the Messiah.

This re-admission into the country, a blessing to Abraham's descendants, began to change the British Empire.

God began to bless a nation whose foundation was built on piracy and slavery. Two and a half centuries later (1919) the Brits would receive a mandate in Palestine. At the 1919 Paris Peace Conference, the Zionist organization made the following proposal:

"We ask that Great Britain shall act as Mandatory of the League of Nations for Palestine... The preference on the part of the Jews for a British Trusteeship is unquestionably the result of the peculiar relationship of England to the Jewish Palestinian problem. The return of the Jews to Zion has not only been a remarkable feature in English literature, but in the domain of statecraft it has played its part, beginning with the re-admission of the Jews under Cromwell."

Short History of the Jews in England

- 1066: William the Conqueror brought Jews from Rouen (Normandy) to London.
- 1279: Jews ordered to attend sermons delivered by Dominican friars
- 18 July, 1290: Edict expelling Jews by King Edward I
- 31 October, 1655: Address by Menasseh ben Israel to Oliver Cromwell. On 13 November he submitted a petition for the readmission of Jews to England.
- December 1655: Whitehall Conference to discuss the petition. Dissolved by Cromwell before it reached a decision
- 1656: Jewish residents of London began living openly as Jews
- December 1656: First Synagogue established after Readmission
- 1290 - 1656: The period between the expulsion of the Jews in 1290 and their re-admission in 1656 is generally called 'The Middle Period'. The re-admission of the Jews in 1656 under the Cromwellian Protectorate changed the fortunes of the British Isles.

Menasseh ben Israel

Medieval Jews in England

24

Having been officially banned for three and a half centuries, under Cromwell the descendants of Abraham were finally allowed readmission in 1656. There was a change - something was happening, even though the people living at that time didn't notice it. It took a godly man like Cromwell, who was no Sunday-school teacher but a tough soldier, to play a key part in the plan that God always had for His people and for those who helped them.

Cromwell was a firm believer in "Providentialism", which meant that God was actively involved and directing the affairs of the world. He was doing this through the actions of certain "chosen people" (whom God 'had provided' for such purposes). Obviously, Cromwell saw himself as one of the 'chosen' and he had to play his part.

Some Jewish people were permitted to rise to the highest levels, but it took another 212 years for a Jew to finally become Prime Minister (although he was a convert to Christianity) - **Benjamin Disraeli** served Britain in 1868 and again from 1874- 1880.

Other Bible-believing men and women in England greatly contributed to the rise of the empire.

Benjamin Disraeli

John Newton

(1725 –1807) was a clergyman and former slave-ship captain who transported slaves from Africa to the Americas and England. Imprisoned slaves on his ships who died en-route were tossed overboard. Newton left the slavery business and became a truly changed Christian and a preacher. Today, we continue to sing the songs he wrote, such as "Amazing Grace". Most importantly, he wrote about the slave trade and how his life and views had been changed since he played a part in that horrible enterprise.

John Newton

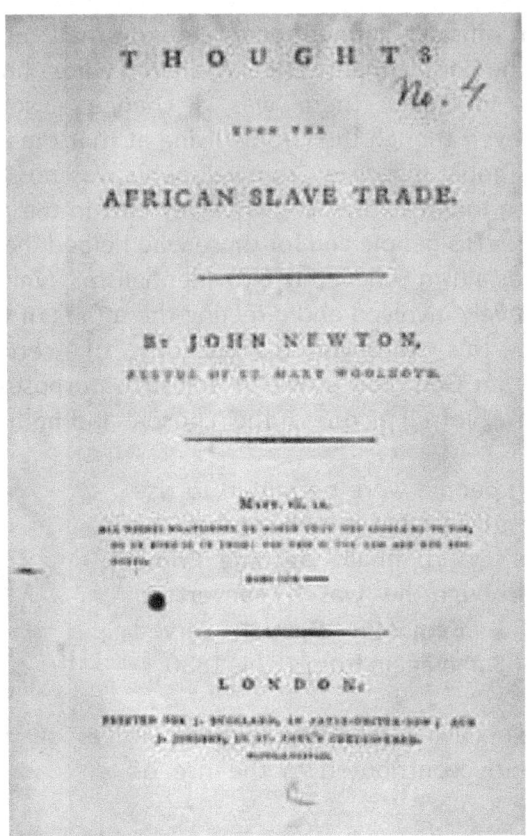

One man's passion to right the wrong he had been involved in and the power of the message in his tract demanding the abolition of slavery, "Thoughts Upon the African Slave Trade" was extremely influential in challenging and eventually changing the hearts of many in the British Empire. It graphically described the horrors of the Slave Trade and his role in it.

Newton's stand on this issue influenced many people, but none were as committed as a young politician who seemed destined to become Prime minister - **William Wilberforce** (1759-1833).

After becoming a believer in 1785, Wilberforce wanted to quit politics and enter the ministry. John Newton, however, reminded him of what he could accomplish nationally if he remained in the government. He was also encouraged and inspired by many supporters who told him, "We simply cannot be in this horrible ungodly slave business. This is not right in God's eyes, Wilberforce,

❝

A private faith that does not act in the face of oppression is no faith at all.

William Wilberforce

you now are a believer and you've got to take a stand. God has elevated you to your position for a vital reason. You must play out your part in this great drama."

By the late 1700s, the economics of slavery were so entrenched in the English economy that only a handful of people thought anything could ever be done about it. For decades, the British government

A LETTER

ON

THE ABOLITION

OF THE

SLAVE TRADE;

ADDRESSED TO THE

FREEHOLDERS AND OTHER INHABITANTS

OF

YORKSHIRE.

By W. WILBERFORCE, Esq.

"There is neither Greek nor Jew, circumcision nor uncircumcision, Barbarian, Scythian, bond nor free: but Christ is all, and in all. Put on therefore bowels of mercies, kindness," &c.—Col. iii. 11, 12.

"God hath made of one blood all nations of men, for to dwell on all the face of the earth."—Acts xvii. 26.

LONDON:

Printed by Luke Hansard & Sons,

FOR T. CADELL AND W. DAVIES, STRAND; AND J. HATCHARD, PICCADILLY.

1807.

itself had become enslaved to the monetary benefits of the slave trade. Being the only abolitionist in Parliament, Wilberforce started introducing bills to end the slavery. Again and again, with each new parliamentary year, Wilberforce reintroduced the Abolition papers. He never gave up, he persevered and gradually, he won over a couple of Members of Parliament.

For 26 years, Wilberforce headed the campaign against the British slave trade until the passage of the Slave Trade Act 1807. Despite its fine-sounding-title, it did not end slavery.

"Am I not a Man and a Brother?"

The ceramic 'slave medallion', made by Wedgwood for the Society for the Abolition of the Slave Trade in 1787, became a very important symbol. This slave, of whom many people believed to be only half human, asks them, "Am I not a man also? Am I not like you?"

This question touched the hearts and conscience of the British people. Gradually, they began to see that slavery was leading the society into an amoral and ungodly proposition.

However, slavery was finally abolished in the British Empire with the Slavery Abolition Act of 1833 - ironically it was also the year of Wilberforce's death. The Providentialists would certainly have proclaimed that William Wilberforce had faithfully played out his God-assigned role.

> *"You may choose to look the other way, but you can never say again that you did not know."*
> **Wilberforce**

Not only did Britain outlaw slavery, but in their newfound enthusiasm they began attacking slave ships from other countries.

The abolition of slavery was undoubtedly one of the great moral turning events in the history of the world.

One man, William Wilberforce, helped change the course of a nation and eventually the course of an empire!

Jewish People Impacting the British Empire

Sir Moses Haim Montefiore (1784-1885) was a financier, banker, and most prominently a major philanthropist dedicated to helping the poor destitute Jews of Jerusalem. He also worked closely with organizations that were dedicated to the abolition of slavery. Even Christian churches and hospitals were recipients of his charity. His philanthropic projects made him the most famous British Jew of the Empire and even today, more than 130 years after his death, his reputation remains intact. Some of the projects he started (such as an orchard and a school for

The centenary of Sir Moses Montefiore 1884

agricultural training and workshops and neighborhoods outside the walls of the Old City) laid the foundations for the first of the waves of immigration that followed 40 years later. By building a windmill, the great benefactor hoped to entice the Jews huddling inside the Walls of the Old City to come out and live and productively work in much more sanitary conditions. Some did, but most would scurry back into the Old City at night because they felt safer there. Today those small neighborhoods are some of the most sought after and uniquely beautiful historical residential areas of Jerusalem. He made seven arduous and extremely dangerous voyages by ship and carriage to the Holy Land. His last tour was at the age of 91. There is little doubt that he was used by God as one of the foundational stepping stones for the return of the Jewish people to the Promised Land. By marriage he was related to the British Rothschild family which was also extremely influential in British and Zionist work.

Montefiore lived to be over 100 years old and was honored by being referred to as the "grand old Hebrew". He was the second Jew in history ever to be knighted and among other honors, he even found time to serve as the Sheriff of London. I wonder if any Londoner at the time ever referred to the Hebrew lawman by exclaiming, "Wow! There's a new Sheriff in town."

Benjamin Disraeli (1804 –1881) was a British Prime Minister, parliamentarian, conservative statesman and literary figure who served in the government for three decades, twice as Prime Minister.

Benjamin Disraeli (*D'Israel* – from Israel) came from a Jewish family who had converted to Christianity when Benjamin was a child. Although he was a devout and practicing Christian, it is apparent by the books he authored that he had a Jewish heart. He was one of the geniuses who envisioned that Britain could become a world-wide empire. One of the most daring things he did personally (without the authorization of the Parliament) was to make a surprise purchase in 1875 of nearly half the total shares in the Suez Canal Company. Because Parliament was not in session, Disraeli borrowed £4,000,000 from the Rothschilds to purchase the stock before it went off the market. Disraeli knew that control of the Suez Canal would give Britain a much shorter and safer passage to India and would ensure their economic advantage over rivals France and Russia. It was the stroke of a bold genius that eventually made Britain the largest Empire in world history.

THE LION'S SHARE.

"GARE À QUI LA TOUCHE!"

More About Benjamin Disraeli

Benjamin Disraeli was born in 1804 in London to Italian-Jewish parents, just as Moses Montefiore was. His father's dispute with his local synagogue caused him to renounce Judaism and to have his son baptized into the Anglican faith at age 12. The baptism was a formality at the time, but it was pregnant with massive significance for the future of young Benjamin and the Empire.

Benjamin's early business ventures all failed, leaving him heavily in debt and contributing to a nervous breakdown and a long multi-year recovery. Although he was already a published novelist, he became determined to pursue a political career. He failed to be elected in his first three attempts for office, but his persistence finally paid off on the fourth campaign in 1837. Throughout the next 31 years, he experienced many personal setbacks which seemed to doom him to political obscurity as a "back-bencher" in the House of Commons.

"Though I sit down now, the time will come when you will hear me," Disraeli's maiden speech - 1837

However, in 1847 a small political crisis occurred. In that year's general election, Lionel de Rothschild was elected to Parliament. As a practicing Jew, Rothschild was unable to take the oath of allegiance using the prescribed Christian format, and therefore he could not take his seat.

It was proposed that the oath should be amended to permit Jews to enter Parliament.

> *"One secret of success in life is for a man to be ready for his opportunity when it comes." Benjamin Disraeli*

Disraeli spoke in favor of the measure, arguing that Christianity was "completed Judaism", and asking the House of Commons, "Where is your Christianity if you do not believe in their Judaism?"

Although he was briefly elevated to Prime Minister in a caretaker government of 1868, he was quickly removed from office in less than a year.

Cartoon of Disraeli's political climb to power

He went back into the wilderness of the opposition for the next five years. However, at the advanced age (in those days) of 70 he again entered #10 Downing Street as Prime Minister. It was a long, tricky and slippery climb on what he described as "the greased pole" of British politics. He is the only British prime minister to have been of Jewish birth and the first person from an ethnic minority background to twice hold the premiership.

Meanwhile, Britain's greatest rival France obtained a concession from the viceroy of Egypt to construct a canal linking the Mediterranean with the Indian Ocean and open to ships of all nations.

The stock-funded company was to operate the canal by leasing the relevant land for 99 years from its opening. The Suez Canal Company came into being in December 1858. Disraeli perceived the French project as a threat to Britain's (or at least to his) geopolitical and financial goals.

Initially, international opinion was skeptical about the project and Suez Canal Company shares did not sell well overseas. Britain, the United States, Austria and Russia did not even buy any shares, although all French shares were quickly sold out in France. The canal opened to shipping on 17 November 1869, and had an immediate and dramatic effect on world trade, playing an important role in increasing European penetration and colonization of Africa. External debts and profligate spending forced Isma'il Pasha, the Egyptian Khedive to put up his country's shares for sale.

When Disraeli was informed that the shares were available, he acted alone in a matter of hours, without consulting Parliament. The London banking house of Rothschild & Sons advanced to the Prime Minister, acting for the British Government, £4,000,000 to purchase Suez Canal shares. Disraeli was a close personal friend of Lionel de Rothschild, and according to legend, this was transacted on a gentleman's agreement.

European governments were highly impressed, while others were alarmed seeing the action as evidence that Britain had finally abandoned her passivity and was embarking upon a new and robust foreign policy which would eventually elevate her to ruling over the largest empire in world history. The control of the canal marked a new policy that extended British commitment in Egypt, along with ensuring the imperial lifeline to India and Australia and effectively ensuring that world trade routes would not be controlled by France. In the years to come, the security of the Suez Canal as the pathway to India became a major focus of British Foreign policy. The Balfour Declaration of 1917 some 40 years in the future was heavily influenced by ensuring the security of the canal. Some advocates proposed that if the Jews were ensconced in Palestine, they would be loyal to the British and help to protect 'The Big Ditch'. In fact, the Israeli Army was used for that very purpose in the 1956 Sinai Campaign some 80 years into the future.

"CONSERVATISM discards PRESCRIPTION, shrinks from PRINCIPLE, disavows PROGRESS; having rejected all respect for antiquity, it offers no redress for the PRESENT and makes no preparation for the FUTURE." **Benjamin Disraeli**

"The view of Jerusalem is the history of the world; it is more, it is the history of earth and of heaven." **Benjamin Disraeli**

In a free-wheeling debate the point may well be taken that Benjamin Disraeli was also a founding father of the future Jewish State. (Actually I've never heard anyone make that argument...so if I ever get into doing footnotes I'll have to give that one to myself.)

Disraeli was a lot like President Trump: he didn't try 'old school' diplomacy and he didn't go to the parliament and let them debate and talk the purchase to death. From experience he knew that the London political windbags would slowly smother the idea if he brought up the subject. Instead, he acted, went back to Parliament and said, "Guess what I just bought?"

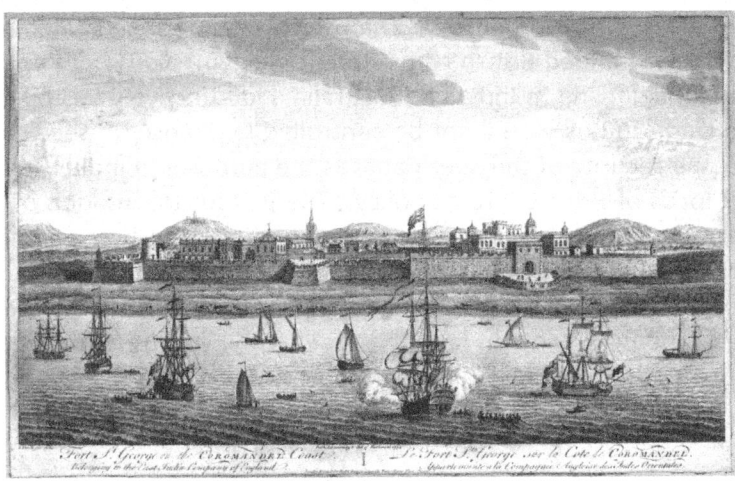

Purchasing the Suez Canal changed everything and gave the world a new phrase, "Mideast." This term only made sense to the British leaders who were looking toward the east (which meant India) - the future crown Jewel of Disraeli's envisioned empire. The canal was mid way there, so the region began to be called the Mid or Middle East.

I believe that God put men like Benjamin Disraeli in that high position. Isn't it interesting that this son of Abraham, a believer, became the architect of the largest empire in world history?

When England began to be a blessing to the Jews and allowed them to be free to worship and to participate in governmental affairs, that little English island blossomed into a worldwide empire.

CHAPTER 6
The Sun Never Sets on the British Empire

The expression, "The sun never sets on the British Empire" came into being because the Empire stretched all the way around the globe from New Zealand, across Australia to India, across Africa and Canada. Nothing like this had ever happened before in the history of the world. The British Empire was made up of colonies, protectorates, dominions, and mandates administered by the United Kingdom. By 1913, the Empire had more than 412 million people. This was almost a quarter of the global population. In 1917, at the peak of British expansion, Britain did something that was again a blessing to the Jewish people. It was the **Balfour Declaration.**

Sir Arthur Balfour (1848 –1930) had a long and distinguished political career. He was Prime Minister (1902-1905) and during World War I, he served as the Empire's Foreign Secretary. Prime Minster David Lloyd George and Balfour, two men who couldn't have been more different, served together during WWI.

Aristocratic Balfour was groomed to be a Prime Minister, following in the footsteps of his uncle Lord Salisbury who had also served as Premier. But unlike many aristocrats, Balfour's Bible-believing mother raised him on the tenets of Scripture. Balfour never married, but the lady closest to him was his niece, Blanche Dugdale (known to all the family insiders as "Baffy", a play on words on her maiden name "Balfour". She was totally committed to the Zionist cause and to her uncle. "Baffy" authored a two-volume biography of her uncle that revealed so much of Sir Arthur's character, habits and interests. In her own right, she was a blessing to the Jews and described by Chaim Weismann as "an ardent lifelong friend of Zionism."

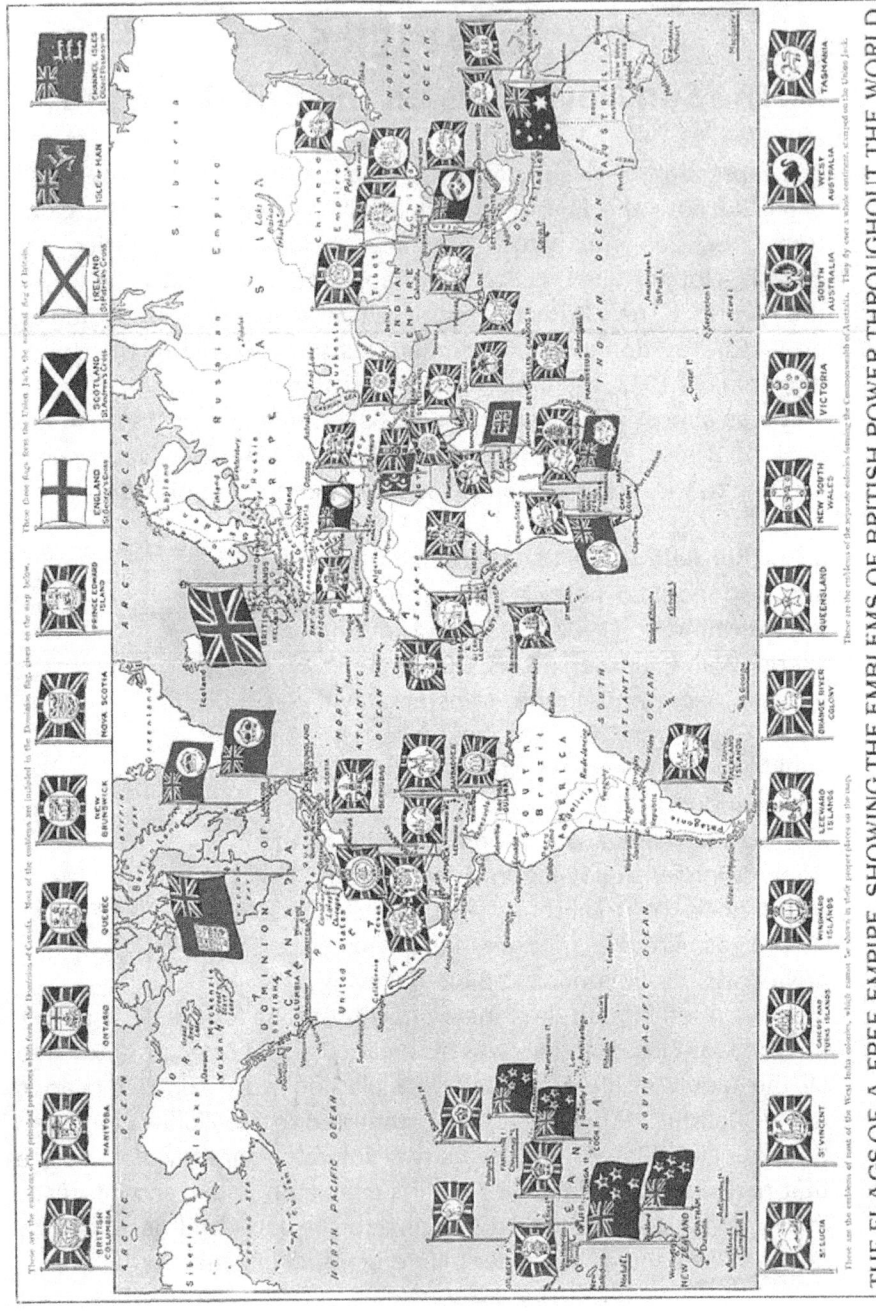

THE FLAGS OF A FREE EMPIRE, SHOWING THE EMBLEMS OF BRITISH POWER THROUGHOUT THE WORLD

She passed away on the 16th of May, 1948 just a day after hearing the good news that the state of Israel had been declared.

Balfour had many interests, as attested to by the myriad of open books spread throughout his home. There were always open Bibles spread throughout his mansion as well. Unlike the other strictly political lawmakers, it was Balfour who had a steady scriptural rudder attempting to set the course for the ship of state. His mother's early and consistent Biblically based guidance rubbed off on a nation.

David Lloyd-George (1863 –1945) was a rough and tumble lawyer, a street hustler and someone who today would be called "an ambulance chaser". The duplicity and switching of loyalties was the coin of the in-fighting of 19th century politics. (Has anything really changed?)

However, God, with His wonderful sense of humor and timing, saw that Lloyd George was elevated from the nearly dead pile of previously rejected politicians to become Britain's Prime Minster during the depths of the Great War, and Arthur Balfour was appointed the wartime Foreign Secretary. Incredibly, both men had a Biblical background and Godly seeds had been planted in their hearts in childhood.

I can just see little Davey, making the trek with his widowed mother and his siblings after his father's untimely death at age 44, back to his mother's hometown in Wales. It was in this small village that Davey acquired most of his political views, especially his hatred of the large landowning aristocracy. These liberal positions were adamantly held and espoused by his mother's family.

> *"Don't be afraid to take a big step if one is indicated. You can't cross a chasm in two small jumps."*
> **David Lloyd George**

David George's uncle, Richard Lloyd (1834–1917), was a shoemaker, a minister (in the Scotch Baptists and then the Church of Christ) movement in Wales.

Uncle Richard was a towering influence, encouraging Davey to take up a career in law and to enter politics. Little Davey, whose mother tongue was Welsh, was so impressed by his uncle Richard that he even added his uncle's surname to his to become "David Lloyd George". Picture that little boy standing at the kitchen table where flickering candlelight illuminated the open Bible. I can almost see his uncle's pointing at the Bible verses and thrilling the little boy when he thundered his deeply held belief, "Davey, someday, mark my words, the Jews have to go back to the God-given holy land of Israel. Don't ever let any heathen talk you out of that!"

This truth was repeatedly poured into that little head.

Eventually, David became a lawyer and entered politics. His political antics (stabbing opponents in the back, extreme liberalism, anti-church of England, anti-Boer War, etc.) alienated many. When the possibility of defeat in the Great War loomed, a true fighter was needed to awaken the country and lead the fight for survival. The time had come to dismiss Prime Minister Asquith, the smooth politician, and call in the backroom brawler. Twenty-four years later, a similar situation occurred when Winston Churchill replaced 'the Great Appeaser' Neville Chamberlain to lead the country during the Second World War.

As Lloyd George rose to the occasion, a handful of Bible-believing politicians bolstered the idea of helping the Jews return to their God-given homeland. We have just seen how the ideas to be a blessing to the Jews were planted in childhood into the heart of Lloyd George, but how did the pieces fall that propelled him into the leadership of the nation?

Herbert H. Asquith was the Prime Minister starting in 1908, and he certainly intended to remain in power until the First World War was concluded. But Asquith had no interest in Jewish affairs or in getting a mandate for Palestine.

As a matter of fact, he had an overwhelming reason **not** to do anything that would be a blessing to the Jews. Asquith was well known in those days as a 'skirt-chaser.' When he entered the Prime Minister's office he continued his habits, but this married man in his 60s with seven children fell hopelessly in love with a girlfriend of his daughter's who was in her twenties. Their affair lasted sometime and he had the habit of writing her several times a day with pretty revealing thoughts and state secrets. Her name was Venetia Stanley, and she kept all of his letters.

Herbert H. Asquith

He also revealed state secrets, and asked her advice on most issues. He was extremely indiscreet with state secrets especially in wartime.

On the 12th of May 1915, he received a *'Dear John'* letter from Venetia, informing him that the affair was over and that she had decided to marry his Jewish protege Edwin Montagu. Strangely enough there was a Cabinet meeting in session where both men at opposite ends of the table were both writing to Venetia. Asquith pleaded, "This is too terrible.... No hell can be so bad. Cannot you send me one word?... It is so unnatural.... Only one word?"

His attention to his work and other responsibilities started to fail. His weakness as a war leader became more evident, and this former master politician seemed to have lost his skills and his enthusiasm for the task. Meanwhile, his broken heart and the animosity against his Jewish rival all contributed to his political downfall.

In the background Lloyd George was organizing his own political overthrow of the P.M. when he smelled blood in the water and eventually replaced Asquith as Prime Minister in December 1916.

If truth be told, Lloyd-George was just as big a 'skirt-chaser' as his predecessor, but he had one thing going for him. He was God's man for the task of midwife to the Balfour Declaration and Asquith was not. Isn't it amazing that sometimes it takes a century to find all the pieces to the puzzle and then you see how God has always been working out his plan?

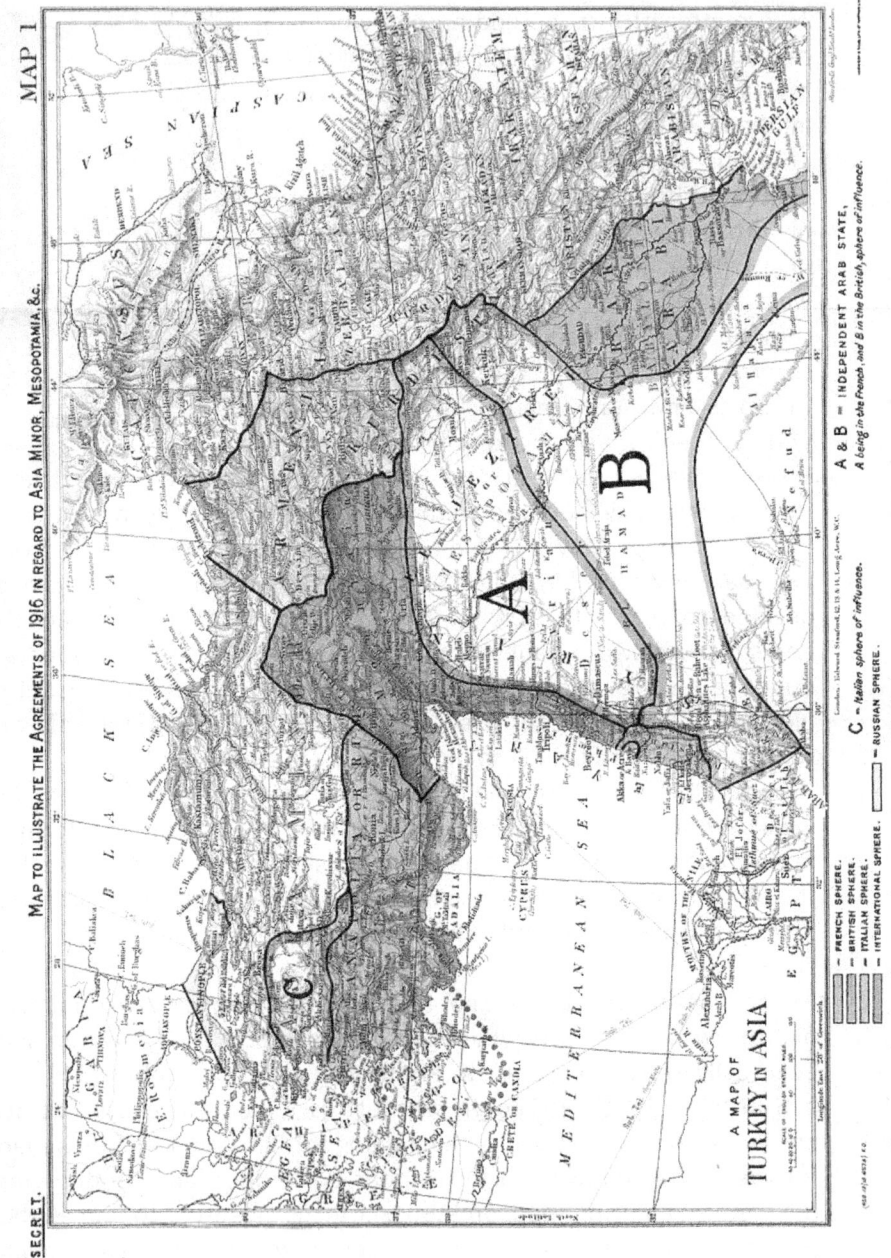

In 1931, Dr. Chaim Weizmann, the President of the Zionist Organization and much later, the 1st President of Israel, described David Lloyd George as,

"...a great son of a small people. He comes from the hills of Wales, so similar to the hills of Judea; reared in the traditions of the Bible and the Prophets. Intuitively he understood the essentials of the Zionist movement coupled with the tribulations of the Jewish people in the war and from that moment he has been the devoted friend of the (Zionist) movement and has placed the Jewish people under a heavy debt of gratitude. He not only initiated the Balfour Declaration but followed the development of the Zionist movement and the upbuilding of Palestine with keen and friendly interest in every stage."

It's amazing to see how several very different men from a variety of backgrounds became united around the concept to become the biggest blessing to Abraham's descendants since the time of King Cyrus.

The idea to become the nation that is a blessing to the Jews seemed to have been at least a small part of the larger concept of the Balfour Declaration. Together with Jews from around the world, these British government officials planned to return all the land which has been denied to them for millennia.

They decided, "When this Great War is over, we are going to slice and cut up the Ottoman Empire. We're going to take back from the Turks what used to be Israel. Those Ottoman Turks have tramped on it and ruined it for 400 years."

As predicted, at the end of The Great War (WW1), all that remained of the giant old bird (Ottoman Empire) was a country called Turkey. In the end, Britain disengaged itself from the **Sykes-Picot Agreement** but eventually it got the land that used to be Israel. That was a blessing to the Jews.

> The Sykes–Picot Agreement (or Asia Minor Agreement) was a secret 1916 agreement between the United Kingdom and France, to which the Russian Empire assented. It defined mutually agreed spheres of influence and control in Southwestern Asia. The deal is still mentioned when considering the region and its present-day conflicts.

Martin Kramer's article in the June 2017 edition of *Mosaic* summarized the importance of the Balfour Declaration by succinctly combining the elements of all the previous groundwork that went into the document:

"The Balfour Declaration wasn't the isolated act of one nation. It was approved in advance by the Allied powers whose consensus then constituted the only source of international legitimacy. Before Balfour signed his declaration, leaders and statesmen of other democratic nations signed their names on similar letters and assurances. The Balfour Declaration anticipated a world regulated by a consortium of principal powers—the same world that, 30 years later, would pass a UN Resolution legitimizing the establishment of a Jewish state….The poetic simplicity of the Balfour Declaration resides in its presumption that a home for the Jews in their land needs no justification."

Recall Joel 3:2 where God says,

"I'm going to judge nations if they divide my land."

Foreign Office,
November 2nd, 1917.

Dear Lord Rothschild,

I have much pleasure in conveying to you, on behalf of His Majesty's Government, the following declaration of sympathy with Jewish Zionist aspirations which has been submitted to. and approved by, the Cabinet

'His Majesty's Government view with favour the establishment in Palestine of a national home for the Jewish people. and will use their best endeavours to facilitate the achievement of this object. it being clearly understood that nothing shall be done which may prejudice the civil and religious rights of existing non-Jewish communities in Palestine, or the rights and political status enjoyed by Jews in any other country'

I should be grateful if you would bring this declaration to the knowledge of the Zionist Federation.

Yours

Arthur James Balfour

PALESTINE FOR THE JEWS.

OFFICIAL SYMPATHY.

Mr. Balfour has sent the following letter to Lord Rothschild in regard to the establishment of a national home in Palestine for the Jewish people :—

I have much pleasure in conveying to you, on behalf of his Majesty's Government, the following declaration of sympathy with Jewish Zionist aspirations which has been submitted to and approved by the Cabinet :—

His Majesty's Government view with favour the establishment in Palestine of a national home for the Jewish people, and will use their best endeavours to facilitate the achievement of this object, it being clearly understood that nothing shall be done which may prejudice the civil and religious rights of existing non-Jewish communities in Palestine, or the rights and political status enjoyed by Jews in any other country.

I should be grateful if you would bring this declaration to the knowledge of the Zionist Federation.

Times of London, November 9, 1917

CHAPTER 7
A State, a Nation for the Jewish People or a National Home?

The most important thing that emerged from the numerous drafts of the Balfour Declaration was that the British government edged ever closer to help create 'a state which would be the National Home for the Jewish people.'

But then the word-smiths weighed in on the one phrase, 'national home'.

As often happens in diplomacy, terms are used (or invented) so that they are acceptable to all sides. However, people have their own peculiar definitions so that at least they can leave the table with a phrase that is to their liking while at the same time knowing that the other side has a completely different definition in mind.

This charade has happened many times in the slippery lip-craft of international diplomacy.

How is this done?

When it is obvious that no common agreement can be reached because gaps in positions are just too large to bridge, the 'wordsmiths' invent or re-define a complex word or phrase that will be acceptable to both sides if they can keep their own individual definitions. These are classic cases of "kicking the proverbial can down the road" so someone can deal with the future consequences.

Photos of diplomats shaking hands and smiling at each other signifies, not that the disagreements were solved, but that they found a phrase that will paper-over the differences and leave the problem for future negotiators.

As an example, what does "His Majesty's Government view with favor the establishment in Palestine of a 'national home' for the Jewish people" really mean?

Unpacking that statement, one should ask,

1.   What was meant by 'a national home'?
2.   What was the size of that national home?
3.   What were the borders and restrictions of the national home?
4.   Is a national home the same as a state?
5.   Is a state the same as a country or a nation?
6.   What is a national home synonymous with?
7.   Did a national home allow it to be a regular member of the newly organized League of Nations?

Nevertheless, those British leaders brought forth something that was of great benefit to the Jewish people. God had been calling those children of Abraham home even before this announcement, for already in the late 1800's, Jews started trickling back into the land.

The term **"National Home"** was first used by the Balfour Declaration in 1917. Its meaning then and now remains clearly intentionally vague and ambiguous. It obviously was chosen because at the time it had no precedent in international law. Its meaning was foggy and unclear (intentionally) when compared to a well-known term such as "state". The term was intentionally used instead of "state" because of opposition to the Zionist program within the British Cabinet.

Oddly enough, the fight against declaring a state for the Jews was led not by some anti-Semites but by a Jewish member of Lloyd George's Cabinet. **Edwin Montagu** was the Secretary of State for India and a practicing Jew who adamantly opposed Zionism and especially the Balfour Declaration. His opposition to it all was manifestly clear in his note to the cabinet, which caused the re-writing of the phrase "Jewish State" into the "national home" and the addition of the protection statements for non-Jews.

Edwin Montagu

The following is one of Montagu's notes to the cabinet:

In a letter to Balfour and the Cabinet he wrote,

"I assert that there is not a Jewish nation. The members of my family, for instance, who have been in this country for generations, have no sort or kind of community of view or of desire with any Jewish family in any other country beyond the fact that they profess to a greater or less degree the same religion. It is no more true to say that a Christian Englishman and a Christian Frenchman are of the same nation. When the Jews are told that Palestine is their national home, every country will immediately desire to get rid of its Jewish citizens, and you will find a population in Palestine driving out its present inhabitants".

His concern was also for his own political future:

"If Palestine will be the National Home of the Jews – all the voters in my constituency will tell me: "Go Home!!!".

"...I assume that it means that Mahommedans and Christians are to make way for the Jews and that the Jews should be put in all positions of preference and should be peculiarly associated with Palestine in the same way that   England is with the English or France with the French, that Turks and other Mahommedans in Palestine will be regarded as foreigners, just in the same way as Jews will hereafter be treated as foreigners in every country but Palestine. Perhaps also citizenship must be granted only as a result of a religious test."

Was that rant the result of his love and concern for the Mahommedans and other non-Jews, or was it a fear that Jews in other nations (including himself) would be looked at as having dual loyalties or less than total love and loyalty to their home countries? How much of this really had to do with his own societal position and the high office he had attained? Quite a lot, I suspect.

Even as it did in early 1948, many American Jews also opposed the recognition of the new Jewish state because of the same fears. I believe it shows a deep-seated fear or belief that no matter how wealthy, assimilated or ensconced in a high position, there is always the nagging concern that tables could turn on them suddenly and they could lose it all because they are Jewish. Many historic records support that happening. "But not here in my country" they say, which calms them for a moment. But then they remember that Jews said the same thing in Europe in the mid-30s and look what happened to them. And Jews believed the same thing in Spain in 1491...and again, and again and again...

Does it not reveal a secret feeling that they sense deep down that they really are an unusual and chosen people by God himself? Of course a standard Jewish joke was recited by Tevye in 'Fiddler on the Roof' when he said, "I know, I know, we are the Chosen People. But just for once, couldn't You choose someone else?"

I believe that deep down in the heart and psyche, perhaps embedded somehow in the DNA, is the reminder to the Jews that they are different and that they are different for a reason. They have been chosen for something special.

Now whether they believe it or not doesn't change the fear of not fulfilling their intended destiny.

Herbert Samuel

Of course not all Jews, then or now, were in favor of Zionism or even the establishment of the state of Israel. In the Jewish world this is not news, but to the Pro-Israel evangelical Christian this opposition is almost incomprehensible. This emphasizes how far apart we Christians and Jews are from truly and lovingly understanding the others' thinking, beliefs, aspirations and fears.

Another member of that war-time cabinet, Sir Herbert Samuel, was not only Jewish but a first cousin of Montagu. Samuel was a moderate Zionist politically who later was appointed as the first High Commissioner of the British Mandate of Palestine. Those cousinly family dinners were either very lively or perhaps were preceded by the announcement I encountered at a Shabbat Dinner in Jerusalem, "Okay, from now on this evening, NO POLITICS will be discussed. Let's eat!"

In summary, it is apparent that the wording 'homeland for the Jews' was a carefully selected phrase that grew out of a compromise between those Ministers who envisioned the ultimate establishment of a Jewish State and those who did not.

For more than a century the story has been crafted in such a way as to imply that the Declaration was totally a British idea and done solely for the post-war expansion of the empire.

Despite misconceptions, the Balfour Declaration was more than the "game of thrones" move of a single power.

Behind it stood the wartime Allies of Britain, each of whom gave it some momentum forward. United States President Woodrow Wilson had previously and secretly given his backing to the Declaration, but the United States didn't declare war on Germany until 6 April 1917, over two-and-a-half years after the war started. However, our pitiful military unpreparedness didn't allow our troops to enter the combat in Europe until the late spring of 1918.

When London finally issued the Declaration, no one doubted that the Allies stood by Britain's side. It never would have been published if there was the slightest apprehension by the British government that it would affect the coalition of allies or keep the Americans from joining the fight.

The American role deserves some explanation and particular emphasis. Few Americans know that President Wilson secretly approved the Balfour Declaration in advance, or that this approval had a decisive effect in the British cabinet. Without that approval it is reasonable to assume that the British would not have gone ahead. They were in desperate need of the U.S. as an ally on the Western front. The United States never joined the League of Nations, and therefore never ratified the mandate. But in June 1922, the United States Congress passed a joint resolution that reproduced the exact text of the Balfour Declaration ("the United States of America favors the establishment in Palestine," etc.). **President Warren G. Harding** signed the resolution the following September.

Warren Gamaliel Harding
(1865 – 1923) was an American politician who served as the 29th President of the United States from 1921 until his death in 1923.

This map shows what the Balfour Declaration outlined to be the size of the national home for the Jewish people.

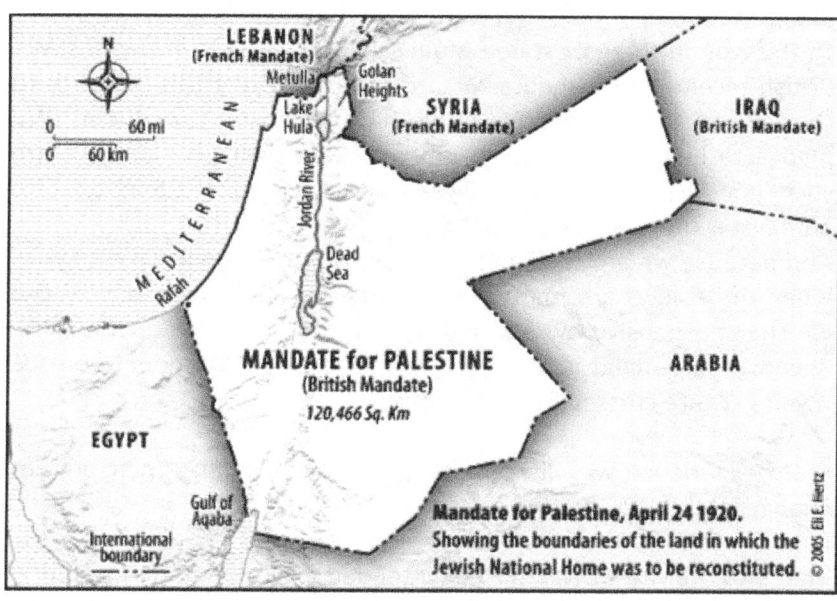

Mandate for Palestine, April 24 1920.
Showing the boundaries of the land in which the Jewish National Home was to be reconstituted.

Size of the Palestine Mandate promised to Israel in 1922	43,000 sq mi
Amount of Palestine Mandate used to form Jordan in 1946	32,500 sq mi
Size of Israel declared by UN in 1948	5,500 sq mi
Size of Israel after the 1949 cease-fire	8,000 sq mi
Size of West Bank and the Golan Heights	2,500 sq mi
Size of Israel after the 1967 cease-fire	10,500 sq mi

As you see when looking at a map of the original British Mandate, it was a big chunk of land. To define the borders, someone put a straight edge on the map and drew in the lines. No cartographer had been out there surveying the area; no one knew if there was a sand dune or a Bedouin encampment or which clan happened to live there. Straight border lines seldom occur naturally but are mainly found on official looking rolls of paper in a far-away-from-reality map room.

Somewhere near the center of the Mandate map is a squiggly line representing the Jordan River connecting the northern Sea of Galilee with the southern end of the waterway - the Dead Sea.

Of this wonderful real estate Britain said, "OK, League of Nations! We British receive the mandate to care for and deliver this property to the Jews of the world because we have reserved it for them. We pledge to help them grow up in it and eventually, because we are such good stewards and mentors, we will teach them how to administer the land and the people.

And because we are such an altruistic government, we will recognize when these Jews are mature enough to run their own country and we shall graciously bow out and return to running our own empire. This mandated land is reserved for the Jews." **NOT!** (Can't you see my fingers are crossed behind my back?)

From experience we all know that governments and their policies change, and Britain was no exception.

The SAN REMO CONFERENCE, attended by Great Britain, France, Italy, and Japan- with the United States as a neutral observer, was held in San Remo, Italy, in April 1920.

Two months earlier, the Allied powers had decided in the London meeting to put Palestine under British Mandatory rule. At San Remo, they confirmed the pledge contained in the Balfour Declaration concerning the establishment of a Jewish national home in Palestine.

Prime Minister David Lloyd George and Lord Curzon represented Britain. Balfour was present as a consultant for final settlement issues. Thanks to British pressure, the French were gradually persuaded to agree to it. Chaim Weizmann, Nahum Sokolow, and Herbert Samuel were also present at the Conference. After a debate, the Balfour Declaration was to be incorporated in Britain's mandate in Palestine. Thus Britain was made responsible "for putting into effect the declaration made on the 8th of November 1917 by the British Government and adopted by the other Allied Powers, in favor of the establishment in Palestine of a national home for the Jewish people; it being clearly understood that nothing should be done which may prejudice the civil and religious rights of existing non-Jewish communities in Palestine, or the rights and political status enjoyed by Jews in any other country."

The exact wording of the 67 word Declaration are repeated because they were adopted verbatim into the League of Nations Mandate.
There was no known mention at the San Remo conference of dividing the mandate into a non-Jewish Arab emirate which would encompass nearly 4/5ths of the original mandate.
After the exhaustion of the 4 year war (1914-1918) in Paris, the victorious allies spent an additional year (1919) in Paris, dividing up the world with new borders where none had existed previously. The Zionists, who had labored so long, were shocked when in 1923 they heard Britain's startling interpretation of the borders of the mandate.

Britain's latest double-dealing with the Jews was the result of years of previous double-dealing, secret pacts, forgotten and unkept promises and cleverly worded letters.

Winston Churchill was the Colonial Secretary given the task of dividing up the land. He made solemn statements to the assembled Arab leaders who had questioned the veracity of British pledges.

Churchill took umbrage at their charges in a paper they submitted to him. He replied,

> "I was sorry to hear in the paper which you have just read that you do not regard that promise as of value. It seems to be a vital matter for you and one to which you should hold most firmly and for the exact fulfillment of which you should claim. If the one promise stands, so does the other; **and we shall be judged** as we faithfully fulfil both....

> "I beg you to realize that we shall strive to be loyal to the promises we have made both to the Arab and to the Jewish people, and that we shall fail neither in the one nor in the other."

Although the redrawing of the map of Palestine is often credited or blamed on Churchill, there is no credible evidence that he actually was responsible for it. The actual banning of Jews across the Jordan was probably determined by those in higher pay levels than Winston's in the early twenties.

The resolution at San Remo was celebrated by mass rallies throughout the Jewish world.

However, in 1921, the British said, "Ah, sorry, little Jews! There's just too much land there for you! We are going to take about 77% of it away from you. You will never need or miss it, because it is on the other side of the Jordan River."
Thus, the British leaders created a brand new *'Judenrein'* (Jew-Free) Arab country on the far side of the Jordan River which they called 'Trans-Jordan'. ('Trans' means the 'other side' or 'across'.)

Maybe you can imagine some of those Church of England British Lords with their hands in the air bursting into a chorus of *"When I looked over Jordan what did I see? A new Arab emirate comin' after me."* This 'song and dance show' was the original 'two-state-solution'.

Imagine for a moment that you are sitting in on the annual board meeting of the 'Two-Staters Solution Inc.' and they are doing a post mortem on the remains of their latest failed solution. "Just a little more tweaking and maybe we are probably or possibly going to get it right next time. After all, gentlemen, it takes patience and perseverance to do basically the same thing over and over and not get the results we promised. Just because it hasn't worked these past 90 years doesn't mean we shouldn't keep trying it again. Let's see if we can get the US to pump a few more measly billion dollars into it. It is bound to get 'lift off' one of these times... and if it doesn't? Of course we have the old fail-safe answer. We'll just blame the Jews again for not wanting to give enough of their land away to the Palestinians. After all, we've had every President since Truman get behind this scheme and eventually Trump will be mesmerized by the sheer beauty of this ultimate deal. Somehow we've got to get 'Mr. Dealmaker' to quit being 'Mr. Troublemaker' and get on board with our fool-proof plan."

Now wasn't that instructive and revealing to hear the inside scoop of what really goes on in those board meetings?

Oh, and by the way, Jimmy Carter, Bill and Hillary and Barack have just been elevated to emeritus status for their life-long achievements for the Two State Cause and in their honor, a nice contribution was made in their names to the Clinton Foundation.

By 1921 on the near-side of Jordan (Palestine), the Brits still allowed Jews to come in, but the population was growing as it mixed with an influx of middle easterners from surrounding lands. The other side of the Jordan, however, was "Arabs only, no Jews allowed!" This British Two State Solution was a new unanticipated wrinkle in the game. This possibility had never been hinted at during the entire year of 1919 in Paris when the Mandates were asked for and the borders were drawn. This was a big change from what the Brits had promised they were going to do when they requested the Mandate for Palestine from the League of Nations.

Actually, it is just how politics has always been played. The rules are posted for all to read. Rule # 1 - Just because we said it doesn't mean we meant it. And it certainly doesn't mean we can't do the exact opposite of what we may have said. Even if we did or did not mean it or say it when we may have said it...or not. Rule # 2 - Forget Rule # 1 whenever you feel the need to. Rule # 3 - Never apologize but always have a good case of 'blame' handy for smearing on the Zionists.

According to the Scriptures we looked at earlier (Genesis 12:3 and Joel 3: 1-2), this behavior is a curse to Abraham's descendants because Britain said, "No Jews allowed to cross the Jordan."
God was very specific about the consequences for cursing His Chosen People and dividing His Promised Land. There will be consequences!

The Brits renamed the two countries Palestine and Transjordan.
That two-state solution lasted from 1923-1948. Besides the 77% of the original plot that was given away, the British continued to divide the land even further. The Golan Heights was given to the French, who also had a Mandate from the League of Nations, and they immediately turned it over to the Syrians.

Originally when Britain controlled the mandated land, they were a blessing to the Jews because they said, "Go back into your historic homeland. We're going to take it over after WWI and you Jews of the world will be ushered into your own ancient homeland." The British government, under Prime Minister Lloyd-George and Foreign Secretary Balfour, was being a blessing to the Jews and they should have expected and anticipated that God would bless them for it. After all...He promised precisely that.

Let's look more closely at how a nation is judged, based on what they do for and to the Jews, both right and wrong.

Halfway to India, or "midway" from England, is the vaunted Suez Canal and the lands surrounding it. I believe that God put men like Benjamin Disraeli in their high position for His purposes.
I find it extremely interesting that this son of Abraham and a Christian believer (all wrapped up in one) became the architect of the largest empire in world history.

When England began to bless the Jews, allowing them to be free to worship and participate in governmental affairs, that little English island blossomed into a worldwide empire.

Besides the 77% of the original plot that was given away, the British leaders continued to divide the land and 'donate' the Golan Heights to the French, who also had a Mandate from the League of Nations. The French immediately turned it over to the Syrians.

"They divided up My Land!"

Great Britain's Division of the Mandate Area, 1921-1923 (First Partition of Palestine)

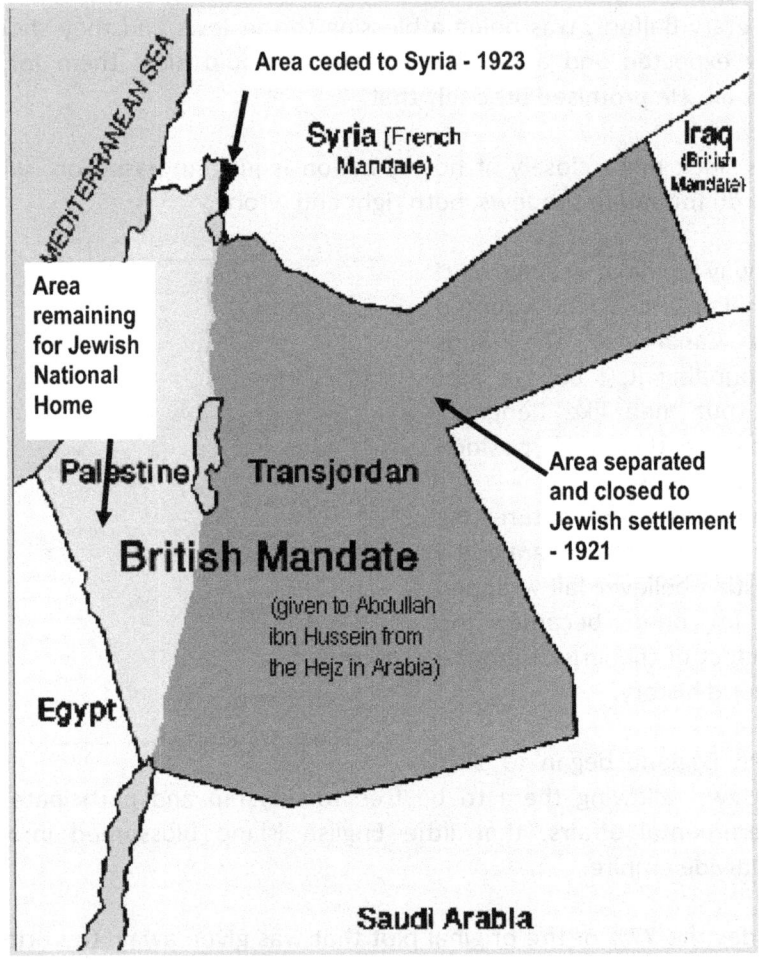

Area ceded to Syria - 1923

Syria (French Mandate)

Iraq (British Mandate)

MEDITERRANEAN SEA

Area remaining for Jewish National Home

Palestine Transjordan

British Mandate

(given to Abdullah ibn Hussein from the Hejz in Arabia)

Area separated and closed to Jewish settlement - 1921

Egypt

Saudi Arabia

"They divided up My Land!"

CHAPTER 8
British Treatment of the Land and the Jewish People

How was the land treated by the British Empire, the largest empire in the history of the world? How did they treat that tiny little piece of property?

They divided it up - the one thing about which God plainly stated, "Don't do that!" (Or as Little Jimmie Dickens said, "You just better not do that.")

The Palestinian Arabs didn't want the Jews entering the country, and neither did many of the British administrators or soldiers stationed there. The majority of those immigrant Arabs were also flooding in unskilled laborers or farm workers. The influx of more and more people caused clashes to erupt between Jews and Arabs which Britain, as the Mandate administrator, tried to resolve (when they felt like it).

Recently, someone asked me: "How can we solve the Arab-Israeli conflict? Are we able to resolve it?" After watching this conflict for more than 40 years myself and reading a ton of its local history, I told him, "The truth is, I don't believe WE can resolve it. This is something in God's hand, something in God's plan."

Each government that comes in and everyone sitting in that White House tried to say: "This is a deal! Somehow, if I can just get these people to sit down at the same table and compromise a little bit, we can solve this." Those people in Washington can't solve anything. Just look at the last several administrations. Republicans sitting across or next to Democrats won't even speak to each other! And yet, somehow, "miracle of miracles" - we think we can take two very diverse people with very different and deeply held prejudices, beliefs, aspirations and religious viewpoints - we are supposed to change their world views and their minds? Give me a break!

We cannot even get politicians in Washington to change their minds on issues or to sit down and compromise on the color of the toilet paper in the congressional bathrooms.

The more we have pushed Israel to divide the land for the new state of Palestine, the more we became complicit in participating in the dividing of the land. God is not mocked. If that action brought down the British Empire, what makes us think we can escape the same consequences?

How did the British treat the people of the Land?
How did they treat God's chosen people?
Remember, Joel 3 says: "Don't mess with my inheritance."
"Don't mess with Texas!" is an interesting statement rolled up into a veiled threat, but it is not as important as when God says, "Don't mess with my inheritance!", by which He means "My people, Israel." Israel is also a Lone Star state (star of David) and just like Texas, it is not to be messed with.

What was going on in Europe at that time?
After Hitler came into power, many of the Jews in Germany rapidly realized, "We have to find a way to get out of Europe!"
Many of them wanted to go to Palestine but the British Government said, "No. We already have too many Jews here and besides, the Arabs don't want you. In the 1939 British White Paper, a yearly quota of 10,000 Jews was approved for the coming five years with the proviso that the Arabs will have to approve any increase above the British arbitrary number." (Fat chance of that ever happening.)

I almost hate to say this, but isn't it a fact that Great Britain has blood on its hands? Millions of desperate Jews who wanted to leave Europe were barred from going to the promised land of Israel. In a way, his Majesty's government said, "No, no! We are going to keep you dispersed... we need to keep you scattered and out of the land you claim is promised to you. You just can't flood in there and upset all the relationships we so carefully constructed with our oil-rich Arab friends. After all, we are the largest and most powerful empire in world history.
Don't you think we know all about maintaining balances of power and prosperity in our world-wide game of thrones? What do you Eastern European Jews bring to the table?

You are the poorest of the poor on the continent. You are incapable of assimilating into our culture. You eat and dress and worship in medieval ways. You always find a way to antagonize the leadership of the countries that have been so kind to host you (like Herr Hitler). It doesn't matter what our previous government promised you under the pressure of the 'Great War' and in accordance with their outdated religious views. Times have changed. Who do you think you are anyway?!"

On behavior like this - scattering the Jews - nations are judged. That is exactly how Britain treated them. Remember that God said: "I'm going to bless those that bless you and curse those that curse you."
Keeping the Jews out of the Promised Land resulted in millions of them ending up in Nazi's gas chambers and therefore, the British Empire called this damnable curse upon their own head.

There is something else that most people don't know about.
Shortly after their rise to power, the Nazis negotiated the **Ha'avara** or **"Transfer" Agreement** with the Jewish Agency.
Although Hitler later attacked England, he seemed to respect their imperial rights and their views of the proper world order.

The August 25, 1933 *Haavara* Agreement - "transfer agreement" was signed between Nazi Germany and Zionist German Jews, making migration possible of approximately 60,000 German Jews and $100 million worth of their assets would be moved to Palestine between 1933–1939. German Jews were able to leave the increasingly hostile Germany while for the Yishuv, the new Jewish community in Palestine, this meant access to both immigrant labor and economic support.

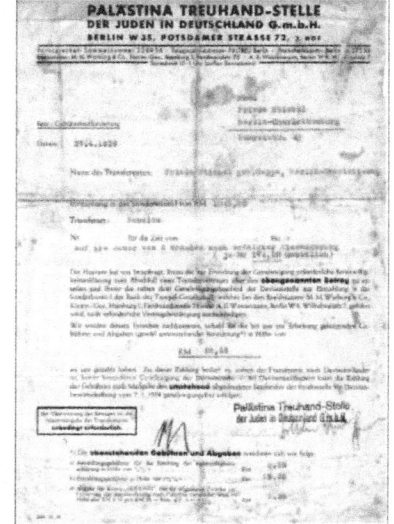

Example of the certificate issued by *Haavara* to Jews emigrating to Palestine.

"The Trust and Transfer Office "*Haavara*" Ltd. places at the disposal of the Banks in Palestine amounts in Reichmarks which have been put at its disposal by the Jewish immigrants from Germany. The Banks avail themselves of these amounts in Reichmarks in order to make payments on behalf of Palestinian merchants for goods imported by them from Germany. The merchants pay in the value of the goods to the Banks and the "*Haavara*" Ltd. pays the countervalue to the Jewish immigrants from Germany. To the same extent that local merchants will make use of this arrangement, the import of German goods will serve to withdraw Jewish capital from Germany. The Trust and Transfer Office, *HAAVARA*, LTD."

The Transfer Agreement (which never actually took place) would recognize British rights in Palestine. It would temporarily refute Arab nationalism and promote Jewish emigration and the transfer of Jewish wealth into the impoverished Palestine, thereby aiding the cash-strapped middle eastern country as well as England.

Hitler even offered the German Jews to Great Britain. "Take these Jews out of Germany," he said. "You can have them for free. At best, there are less than 500,000 in our Fatherland. You have saddled us with impossible reparation payments for the last war. You would be doing us and yourselves a financial favor if you would just relocate them into that barren desert you have in Palestine. You don't want them in your country anymore than we do in ours. Let's make a deal. Take them out of Germany where nobody wants them and open up your gates in Palestine, where they all claim they want to go. It's the perfect solution for you and us. Otherwise we may have to consider a 'final solution' for them ourselves. Do we have a deal?"

German Jews, the 'lucky ones' that were able to leave Germany in time.

63

CHAPTER 9
White Papers and Commissions

Since the end of the First World War, Britain had administered Palestine with instructions from the League of Nations Mandates Commission to "facilitate Jewish immigration". However, when the Arabs began to riot, British policy on immigration became a continual attempt to appease the Arabs with strict limits on the number of Jews to be allowed into Palestine.

The first official governmental paper making an attempt to decipher (or reinterpret) the Balfour Declaration was issued in 1922. Although that particular **White Paper** stated that the Balfour Declaration could not be amended and that the Jews were in Palestine by right, it reduced the area of the Mandate by excluding the land east of the Jordan River. This 'Judenrein' area on the East Bank (of the Jordan River) was allocated to the new Arab emirate of Trans-Jordan. This document also established the heretofore unknown and unscientific principle of "Economic Absorptive

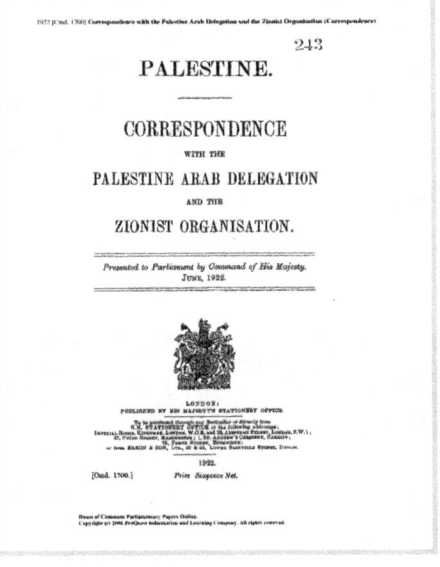

1922 White Paper

Capacity" (EAC) as the main factor for determining the immigration quota of Jews to the West Bank (of the Jordan River) territory of Palestine.

Attempts to limit and slow down the numbers of Jews entering the land were followed by the **Passfield White Paper** of 1930, which was the first attempt to limit Jewish immigration to Palestine.

The **Passfield White Paper,** issued by the Colonial Secretary Lord Passfield (Sidney Webb), was a formal statement of British policy in Palestine made in the aftermath of the 1929 riots. The Hope-Simpson Report had recommended that such a statement be made in the hopes of clarifying unresolved questions concerning the British Mandate for Palestine and the Balfour Declaration. The paper was issued in October, 1930, and like the Hope-Simpson Report, was considered very favorable for the Arabs.

SOLOMON PASSFIELD.
SOLOMON (throwing the £2,500,000 Loan): "Come, come, ladies, never mind the baby. Here's something worth quarrelling about."

While committing to their continued support for a Jewish National Home in Palestine, the Passfield paper's tone was very anti-Jewish. Not only was Jewish immigration limited, there were restrictions on Jewish purchase and ownership of the land and a continual diminution of the available land itself.

Both of these strategies went against Joel 3:2's deadly, "No-Nos" where it emphatically and unambiguously states, "I will enter into judgment against all the nations concerning my People Israel."

"For they scattered my people among the nations (Gentiles) and divided my land."

It started to look like a tag team event by both diminishing the available land area and at the same time progressively restricting Jewish entry into their own homeland. In a nutshell, here we see the deadly pattern that caused the rapid demise of the British Empire; Britain kept God's Chosen People **SCATTERED** and sequentially **DIVIDED** the Promised Land. Reading the history of nations through the prism of God's warnings to nations makes it crystal clear: "Don't Mess with Israel" (neither the People or the Land) unless you are hell-bent on committing national suicide."

The graveyard and junkyard of history is full of nations that tried it.

During the 1936-39 disturbances, a royal commission of inquiry came to Palestine from London to investigate the roots of the Arab-Jewish conflict and to propose solutions. In 1937, after listening to many testimonies, the head of the commission, Lord Robert Peel, issued its recommendations: to abolish the Mandate and partition the country between the two peoples. The British government accepted the recommendations of the Peel Commission regarding the partition of Palestine. Both Jews and Arabs rejected the proposal which ultimately was shelved.

A Jewish bus equipped with wire screens to protect against rocks, grenades and glass throwing, late 1930s

The **White Paper of 1939** was a policy paper issued by the British government under Neville Chamberlain in response to the 1936–39 Arab Revolt. It acted as the governing policy for Mandatory Palestine from 1939 until the British departure in 1948.

The paper called for the establishment of a Jewish national home in an independent Palestinian state within 10 years, rejecting the idea of partitioning Palestine. It also limited Jewish immigration to 50,000 for 5 years, and ruled that further immigration was to be determined by the Arab majority. Restrictions were put on the rights of Jews to buy land from Arabs.

The proposal was rejected by the representatives of Palestine Arab parties and Zionist groups in Palestine. Because of Churchill's opposition and later preoccupation with World War II, this White Paper was never implemented.

PALESTINE

Statement of Policy

1939 White Paper

However, the League Mandates Commission immediately declared the White Paper to be illegal, stating:

"The policy set out in the White Paper is not in accordance with the interpretation which, in agreement with the Mandatory Power and the Council, the Commission has placed upon the Palestine Mandate."

Nevertheless, the British continued to enforce the illegal and outrageous provisions of the 1939 White Paper. By this time though, they had little practical effect since the exit gates for Jews to leave Europe had already been slammed shut.

Long lines of European Jews, desperate to obtain a visa

Just imagine what could have happened if the British Government had taken Hitler's offer of taking the German Jews.

Great Britain would have been a blessing and as a result, God would have abundantly blessed that empire. Their sacrificial efforts would have saved countless lives and even generations of God's Chosen People.

Instead, they became an occupying force in Palestine, hated and attacked by all. In the end, they had to sneak out of the country in the dead of night on the 14th of May, 1948, a defeated and retreating force while their empire slowly stumbled into bankruptcy.

I believe it is important to realize that I have only drawn these conclusions about the fall of the British Empire because of the warnings from Romans 15:4

"For whatsoever things were written aforetime
were written for our learning,
that we through patience
and comfort of the Scriptures
might have hope."

CHAPTER 10
The Esteemed LAND and PEOPLE of Israel

Find out what God has esteemed - the land and the people of Israel.
Don't dis-esteem what God has esteemed!

As an example, let us jump ahead to the end of WWII when Harry Truman was suddenly elevated to the presidency. When the fullness of what had happened to the Jews came to light, Truman was aghast at the horror of the Holocaust. After learning how some of the survivors were being treated under our care in the DP camps, he sent a scathing letter to General Eisenhower to have the abuses corrected immediately. The following quote from the Presidential directive illustrates Truman's feelings on the subject. It is quite a blunt dressing down from a former Army Captain (who was now the Commander-in-Chief) to the 5-Star Supreme Allied Commander.

"As matters now stand, we appear to be treating the Jews as the Nazis treated them except that we do not exterminate them. They are in concentration camps in large numbers under our military guard instead of S.S. troops. One is led to wonder whether the German people, seeing this, are not supposing that we are following or at least condoning Nazi policy."

The Brits and Truman put together an **Anglo-American Committee** which went to Europe and looked at how the Jewish survivors were being forced to live.

The Anglo-American Committee was formed shortly after World War II, following disclosure of horrors of the Holocaust and the problem of refugees and displaced persons. They concluded that only Palestine was willing to accept Jews wishing to leave Europe and recommended that 100,000 immigration certificates be issued immediately. Both the U.S. and British governments would try to find new places for the Displaced Persons. The Mandatory administration was to regulate future immigration to Palestine. The committee's recommendations were accepted by the Jews and rejected by the Arabs. President Harry Truman regarded them favorably, but British Prime Minister Clement Atlee demanded that only after Jewish Resistance, the Haganah, Irgun and Lehi, were disarmed would he provide the 100,000 immigration certificates. The British government continued to carry out its White Paper policy.

DP camp "Kibbutz Buchenwald" in the previous concentration camp

Some Holocaust survivors were being held in Displaced Persons (DP) camps that were the very same camps that the Nazis had imprisoned and tortured them in. Especially in the British sector of occupied Germany, these survivors were still imprisoned, even though the war was now long over.

The committee concluded that no country other than Palestine was ready or willing to help find homes for Jews wishing to leave Europe.

It therefore recommended that 100,000 certificates for immigration to Palestine be issued immediately. Truman agreed and to his great credit, requested and then publicly demanded that Britain release 100,000 Jews from those camps and allow them to go to Palestine.

After giving Truman's demand careful consideration (for about ten minutes), the British leadership publicly and adamantly refused.

◊ **Sh'erit ha-Pletah:** ('the surviving remnant'), following their liberation in the spring of 1945, the Jewish refugees who survived the Holocaust called themselves by this name which was based on Ezra 9:14 and 1 Chronicles 4:43.

◊ **Aliyah Alef** (to go up to Israel) was the 'legal' Jewish immigration. This was an official quota allowed by the British government for Jews to immigrate in small quantities.

◊ **Aliyah Beth,** the illegal immigration according to British Mandate Palestine, began because of the violation of the 1939 "White Paper."

◊ **Ha'apalah** is another name for *Aliyah Beth*. Such a journey began in the refugee camp, via one or two collection points in the American Zone in Germany. From there, the *ma'apalim* (Jews who immigrated illegally to Palestine during British control in the 1930s and 1940s) travelled by truck or train or by foot to the harbors at the Mediterranean Sea.

◊ **The Gesher Bayam** – the bridge over the sea from the *Aliyah Beth* was no less spectacular than the Exodus from Egypt. Jewish refugees reached Eretz Israel by the most unbelievable ways.

Chapter 11
Exodus 1947

Many Jewish survivors, escaping from those shameful and pitiful holding camps, found their way to the south of France.

The *Yishuv* (Palestinian Jewish leadership) had purchased the *SS Warfield,* an old American pleasure cruiser with a shallow draft.

SS Warfield 1946

They planned to take on survivors wanting to go to Palestine and drive it right up on the beach. Then, the survivors could jump off, scatter and be hidden before the British soldiers could catch them. The Jewish leadership was clever in their plans and especially in the re-naming of the ship *Exodus 1947*. In those days, most of the English-speaking world knew what the Exodus connotation meant: the biblical story of the Jews leaving Egyptian slavery and imprisonment and heading toward the freedom of the Promised Land. It didn't take a genius to figure out that Europe had been an even worse Egypt than in Moses' time and that the Promised Land was still in the same place. They were going home, come hell or high water! The British Navy and Air Corps willingly played their parts by replicating a modern-day Pharaoh's Army.

One thousand two hundred and eighty-two women, many of whom were pregnant, 1,600 men and 1,672 children (many orphaned by Nazi atrocities) boarded the ship in Sète, France on July 11, 1947.

As soon as the *Exodus* slipped out of the French harbor, the British chase began and soon got worldwide attention. Newspaper reporters and radio announcers increasingly picked up the story about the air and sea chase across the Mediterranean. The dangerously overloaded ship neared Palestine's shores on July 18.

While the ship was still outside territorial waters, British Destroyers tried to stop the forward motion of the refugee ship.

It was a miracle that only the engines failed from the ramming, for the old ship could have easily sunk, taking 4,500 victims with it. Fighting ensued when British sailors forcibly boarded the ship, killing several people. Among the victims was William Bernstein, an American seaman. The limping ship was towed into Haifa harbor and the survivors unloaded at gunpoint.

Many passengers didn't mind how they were brought to shore: they were too excited that they made it to the Promised Land.

Amongst the passengers were many children who survived the death camps.
They had come home to the one place in the world they thought they'd be welcomed. Instead, they were being herded (again, like cattle) to three prison ships that were waiting for them.

Their British captors told them to wait until the British government had decided their fate.

"These illegal immigrants (Holocaust survivors) are to be deported back to France," was the verdict.

Immigrants from previous 'illegal' ships had been placed in internment camps on Cyprus, a British colony.

Britain's new policy however, served to warn both the Jewish community and European countries assisting in the immigration that these 'illegals' would be sent back to their port of embarkation.

The French government refused to let the British prison ships unload at Port De Bouc.

"No! You can't land them here," they told them. "What you are doing is wrong!"

Because France had been occupied by the Nazis and the Vichy government had collaborated with Hitler, they knew first hand how the Nazis had treated the Jews. This time, they were not going to cooperate with the British maltreatment of the victims. (*Viva la France!*)

Stuck in the French harbor, the passengers began a 24-day hunger strike despite the sweltering summer heat.

This action embarrassed the British government even more.

In the end, the prison ships sailed to the German area temporarily administered by the British. The survivors were brought back to the very people and nation that only recently and efficiently slaught-ered millions of their tribe. In Hamburg harbor, the passengers refused to disembark.

On the pier, an extra loud military band attempted to drown out the screams and cries of the Jewish survivors that were forcibly taken off by British soldiers and dumped into a former German concentration, now detention camp.

"Let the victims of Hitler go to the land of Israel!" Exodus 1947,
written on a barrack in a German DP camp.

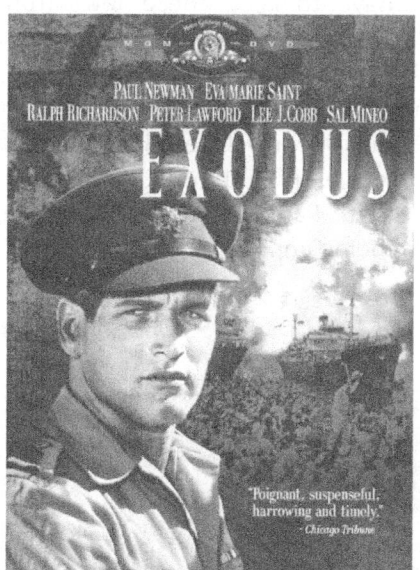

The famous movie *Exodus* with Paul Newman,
made after Leon Uris' book *Exodus*.

Upon hearing the news, all over Europe people in DP camps protested vociferously and staged hunger strikes. Large protests erupted on both sides of the Atlantic.

Britain's public embarrassment played a significant role in the diplomatic swing of sympathy toward the Jews.

By now, Britain realized, "Wow, this was a big PR mistake!"

You can compare it to the 2010 Deepwater Horizon British Petroleum) oil spill off of Louisiana. At first, they thought it was a PR thing, but it turned into a big worldwide condemnation.

Britain then decided, "Okay, we have to keep these Jews from coming into the country. We must keep them scattered. But when we capture them, what are we going to do with them?"

They found a solution by turning much of Cyprus, one of their colonial islands, into a more politically correct terminology - an 'internment camp', which of course was just another name for a 'Jewish prison'. The movie *Exodus* with Paul Newman starts there, where 50,000 Jewish survivors were being imprisoned by the British.

Remember Joel 3? "Don't scatter my people"?

God had drawn these 50,000 people back to their homeland and the British kept them scattered and out of the land. The Cyprus camps operated from August 1946 to January 1949 and in total held about 51,000 Jews. The Brits continued to keep 8,000 military-age men and wives under lock and key, even AFTER Israeli Independence was a fact.

This extended incarceration was to keep the able-bodied young men and women from joining the Israeli Army which was in dire need of troops. It appears that even after the British had resigned their mandate and left the country, they still wanted the Jews to lose the war. It is still another curse piled on top of the others against Abraham's descendants by the British government.

Meanwhile, Britain said, "We're gonna be out of here. Our country is going bankrupt. Everything is going wrong and we can't handle all this fighting." They informed the United Nations, "We are resigning from our Mandate!"

CHAPTER 12
Preparing for War

In the meantime, Britain built the strongest of the Arab armies: the Arab Legion in Trans-Jordan.

The Arab Legion was British equipped, trained and had at least 49 British officers (majors & colonels).

The British Army officers were all "on contract" or "secondment" to an allied military. General John Glubb Pasha led this British-officered Arab army that was ready to attack the Jews the moment a state was declared, which happened to be the same day the British government pulled out of Palestine.

Glubb Pasha in Amman, Jordan

In many ways, that first Arab-Israeli, British-led attack on May 15 was against the very people they promised to assist and protect under the previous day's expired mandate.

Leaving Palestine, Haifa harbor, May 1948

During the 1948-49 Independence War the Egyptians invaded Israel through the Negev Desert. While in the North, the Syrians attacked from the Golan Heights.

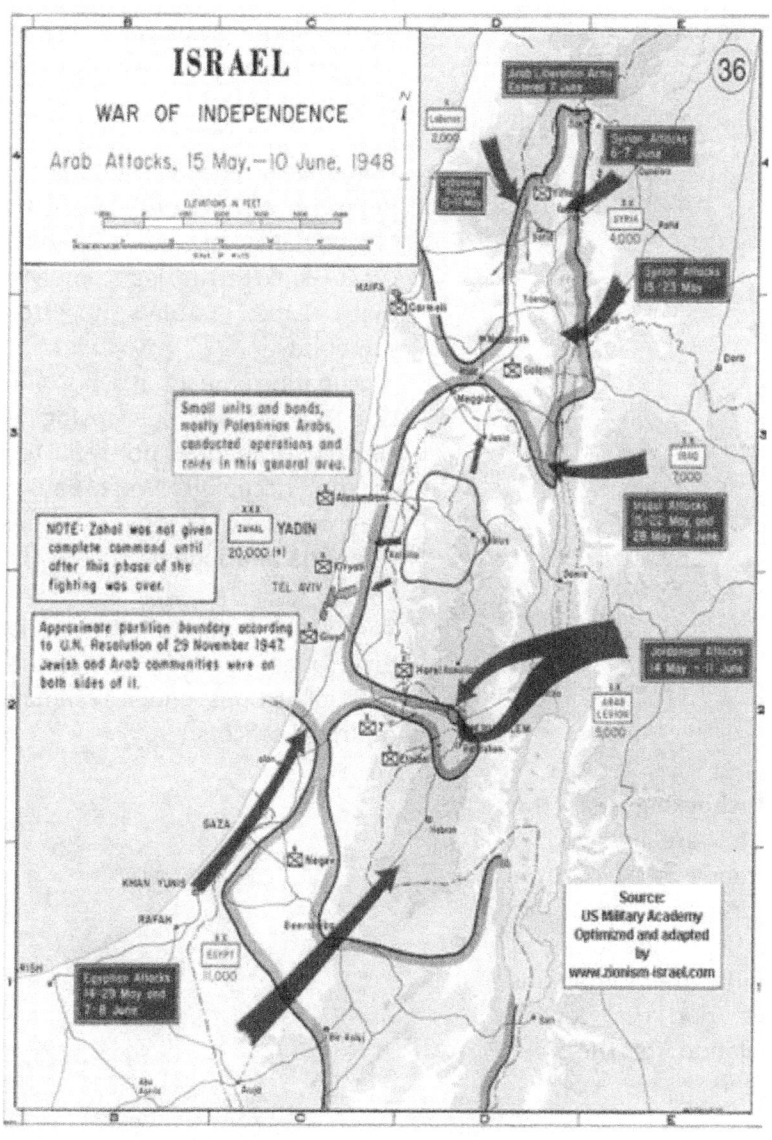

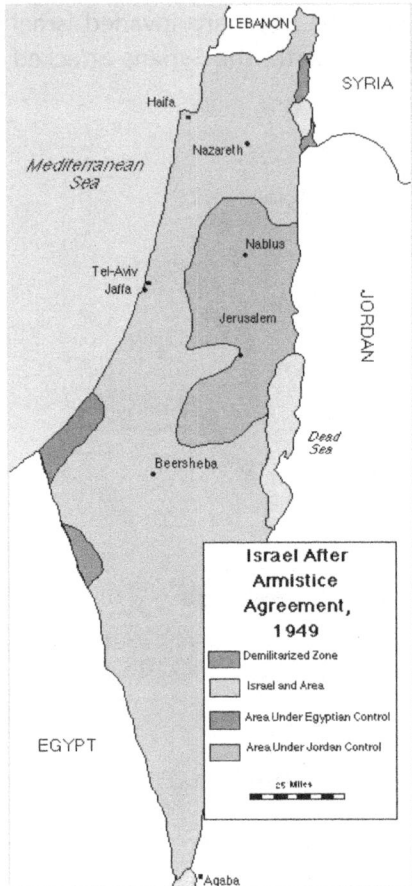

Israel After
Armistice
Agreement,
1949

Demilitarized Zone
Israel and Area
Area Under Egyptian Control
Area Under Jordan Control

25 Miles

Against all odds, Israel fought back and claimed whatever land they could get. It was a free-for-all... nobody owned anything because Britain was gone. That's why this map looks like an omelet.

The Biblical term is "Samaria and Judea", but the world calls it the "West Bank" or the "OCCUPIED West Bank/territories", implying that Israel stole it from somebody.

'Occupation' means it's not your land, you are occupying it illegally. Israel does not refer to it as the 'occupied' West Bank – they call it by its Biblical names: **"Samaria and Judea".**

The West Bank (of the Jordan River) was invaded and occupied by Arab troops under command of British officers.

It is shocking that the British were involved in so many ways. After capturing the Old City of Jerusalem and Judea and Samaria, the Jordanians drove out the Jewish population for the next 19 years.

82

Arab Legion destroying the Old City's Jewish Quarter

Jewish survivors of the Etzion bloc massacre.

From 1948-1967, the 'Judenrein' territory was held by Gentiles, until it was finally liberated in 1967 during the Six Day war.

The Jordanians drove out the Jewish population, including those elderly and disabled Jews from the Jewish Quarter of the Old City in Jerusalem, and the subsequent illegal Jordanian occupation was recognized only by Britain and Pakistan.

JEWS FLEE JUDEA AND SAMARIA AFTER JORDAN ANNEXED THE REGION IN 1948

TODAY, JEWS THAT HAVE RETURNED TO JUDEA AND SAMARIA ARE REFERRED TO AS "ILLEGAL SETTLERS"

Look at the list of all the wars that Israel has had to fight – they can't afford to lose a war. And God will not let them lose a war, either!

List of Israel's Wars and Large-scale Military Operations Since 1948

- 1948 Arab–Israeli War (November 1947 - July 1949) – Civil war between Jewish and Arab militias began during the end of the British Mandate of Palestine. Full scale war erupted when Arab armies invaded Israel.
- Retribution operations (1950s - 1960s) – Constant fedayeen terror attacks were answered by military operations carried out by the IDF. Palestinian militants infiltrated from Syria, Egypt and Jordan into Israel to carry out guerrilla attacks against Israeli civilians and soldiers.
- Suez Crisis (October 1956) – in response to Egypt nationalizing the Suez Canal on July 26, 1956.
- War over Water (November 1964 - May 1967) - Several IDF military operations against Syrian-Lebanese Headwater Diversion Plan, intended to block the flow of the water sources to Israel through the Jordan Valley River Basin and the Sea of Galilee.
- Six-Day War (June 1967) – War against Egypt, Jordan and Syria and troops that were contributed by Iraq, Saudi Arabia, Kuwait, Algeria and others.
- War of Attrition (1968-1970) – Limited war between IDF and forces of the Egyptian Republic, the USSR, Jordan, Syria and the Palestine Liberation Organization from 1967 to 1970, till ceasefire was signed between the countries.
- Yom Kippur War (October 1973) - Fought from October 6 to October 26, 1973 by a coalition of Arab states led by Egypt and Syria against Israel, in a bid to recapture the territory Israel had gained during the Six Day War.
- South Lebanese conflict (March 1978) – also called "Operation Litani". Large-scale IDF invasion of Lebanon, pushing the PLO north of the Litani River.

- Lebanon War (1982) – Also called "Operation Peace for Galilee". The IDF invaded southern Lebanon to expel the PLO from the territory. The war resulted in the expulsion of the PLO from Lebanon and created an Israeli Security Zone in southern Lebanon.
- South Lebanese conflict (1982-2000) - Nearly 20 years of warfare between the Israel Defense Force and its Lebanese proxy militias with Lebanese Muslim guerrillas led by Iranian-backed Hezbollah.
- First Intifada (1987-1993) - First large-scale Palestinian uprising against the so-called Israeli 'occupation' in the Palestinian Territories.
- Second Intifada (2000-2005) - Second Palestinian uprising, a period of intensified violence.
- Lebanon War (summer 2006). IDF response due to constant firing of rockets and cross-border incursions by Hezbollah into Israel. A United Nations-brokered ceasefire went into effect on 14 August 2006. The war formally ended on 8 September 2006.
- Gaza War (December 2008 - January 2009) - Three-week armed conflict between Israel and Hamas. Israel declared an end to the conflict on January 18 and completed its withdrawal on January 21, 2009.
- Gaza War (July - August 2014) Operation Protective Edge, which lasted 50 days, was launched in the Hamas-ruled Gaza Strip. Many terror tunnels were destroyed during this operation.

"We can forgive the Arabs for killing our children. We cannot forgive them for forcing us to kill their children. We will only have peace with the Arabs when they love their children more than they hate us."
Golda Meir

Royal Marine saluting

While I was in the Marine Corps, we had a British Marine training with us who said, "Oh, you US Marines, you are always so concerned about how you salute. You've got all your fingers together and your thumb just right and you make sure that all your troops salute the same way. We British Marines salute like this: slowly up with your hand, and then quickly down."

"What's the significance of that?" I asked him. "It's just like the British Empire. We built an empire slowly, and overnight, it quickly went down."

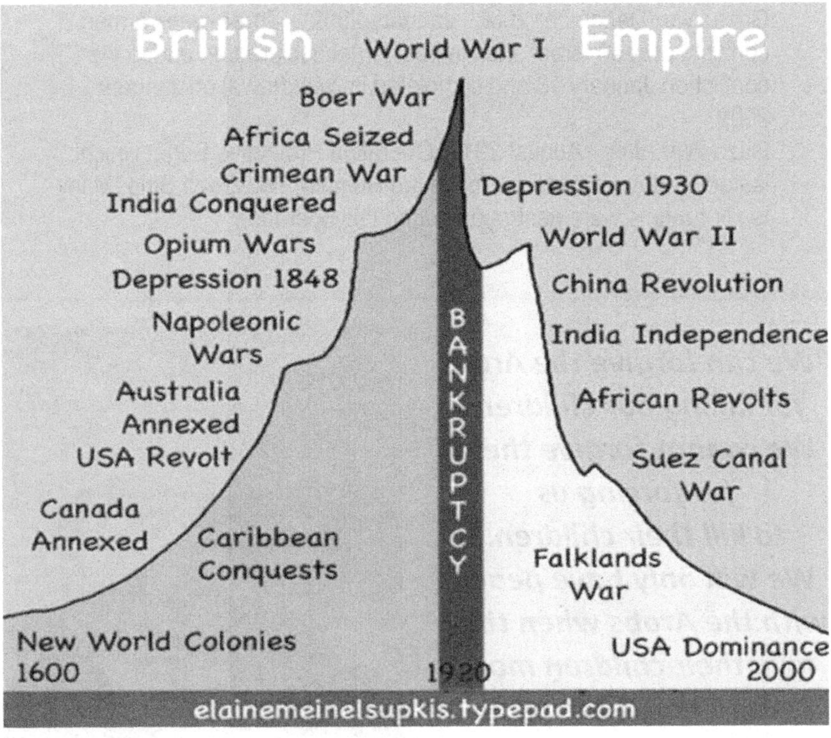

British World War I Empire

Boer War
Africa Seized
Crimean War
India Conquered
Opium Wars
Depression 1848
Napoleonic Wars
Australia Annexed
USA Revolt
Canada Annexed
Caribbean Conquests

Depression 1930
World War II
China Revolution
India Independence
African Revolts
Suez Canal War
Falklands War

BANKRUPTCY

New World Colonies
1600

1920

USA Dominance
2000

elainemeinelsupkis.typepad.com

And that is exactly what happened.

It went down so quickly because they violated and went against God's Word about scattering His People and dividing His Land.

Look at the chart on the left page: It took them about 400 years to build an Empire. Right at the top, between 1917-1921, they started dividing the land of Israel. Then it was just a short way down before the Empire was over.

Why? Because they violated God's Word.

At its height, the British Empire stretched all the way from Australia, across and around the world.

1917: The greatest Empire ever.

By 1947, when the Brits finally pulled out of Palestine and did their worst to Israel, their empire was back to what they were in the year 1200, down to just a few crown-dependent territories.

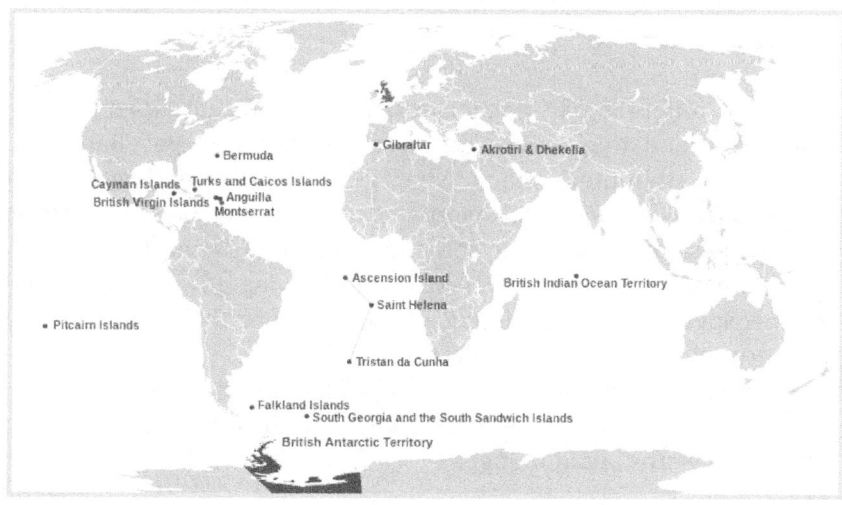

Even though it is still called "the United Kingdom" and people pretend it is still a worldwide empire, it is no longer a world power because everything has fallen apart. Yes, they have nice royal weddings, everybody loves the pomp and ceremony, and they have beautiful royal babies. But that's about the most significant thing that they do today.

Right now, you might be saying to yourself, "Oh no, is he going to make the same point again?" You're darn right I am! After all, this is the main point of the book. Here it comes right down the middle of the plate. God has promised to bless the nation that blesses His chosen people. History has proven that the nations that have blessed the Jewish people have had the blessing of God on them. The nations that have cursed the Jewish people have experienced the curse of God.

> *"If at any time I announce that a nation or kingdom is to be uprooted, torn down and destroyed, and if that nation I warned repents of its evil, then I will relent and not inflict on it the disaster I had planned. And if at another time I announce that a nation or kingdom is to be built up and planted, and if it does evil in my sight and does not obey me, then I will reconsider the good I had intended to do for it."*
>
> Jeremiah 18: 7-10

For years, different USA administrations insisted that Israel should divide their land, to give away the so called 'Occupied West Bank.' We have attempted many strategies to coerce Israel into abandoning their ancestral heartland and have helped develop a neighboring nation which is committed to annihilating Israel from the moment of its birth. Even voluntarily giving any of it away to another sovereign entity is unequivocally "dividing the land." The very act that God specifically forbids! If God judges Gentile nations for doing this, how much worse will it be for the self-same people (Israel) when they divide their holy land which God warns about in Joel 3?

Quartet meeting 2010

If we (the US) apply pressure on Israel to divide their own land (something they wouldn't normally do on their own), are we not responsible for that act of dividing?

Here is an example:

We put a gun in the hand of a small child, tell it to aim at another child and then twist its free arm until the pain forces the child to shoot.

Won't we be the guilty party that forced the incident to happen, even though our fingerprints are not on the weapon?

It is a crude analogy, but doesn't it make the point?

As we had sufficient power to force the crime to happen, we are found guilty of the crime.

"Indifference
is the sign of sickness;
a sickness of the soul
more contagious
than any other."

Elie Wiesel

CHAPTER 13
Missed Opportunities

In recent years even some Israeli governments wanted to do exactly what we and the rest of the world were constantly demanding. The amazing thing is that, again and again, the Palestinian leadership turned down the deals and offers. It seemed that even if they wanted to do so, Israel couldn't give it away.

Following are some 'missed opportunities' for Arabs to have a state of their own.

1.   In 1937 the British Peel Commission concluded that the only logical solution to the contradictory aspirations of the Jews and Arabs was to partition the region into separate Jewish and Arab states. The Arabs totally rejected the proposal because it would have forced them to accept a Jewish state alongside of theirs.
2.   In 1939 the 'British White Paper' proposed the creation of an Arab state and again it was rejected by the Arabs.

Arab or Palestinian?

Not many people know that the flagrant misleading misnomer 'Palestinian' wasn't applied to the Palestinian Arabs until Yasser Arafat came onto the world scene in the 1960s. Prior to May of 1948, the ethnic groups living under the British Mandate resided in the Palestine Mandate. The Jews living in the land of Palestine were accurately described as 'Palestinian Jews' while resident Arabs were described as 'Palestinian Arabs'. Those Arabs identified with their countries of origin and their tribes and clans. They never described themselves as some ethnic people called 'Palestinians' until Arafat convinced the world of a new 'ancient' ethnic group who were homeless and landless. Those 'Palestinians' demanded that the world provide them with a country, because they deserved it!

---

3. In 1947, the UN Partition Plan would have created an Arab state. The Arab response to Israel's acceptance of that UN plan was: the war of 1948-49. It was the Arab aggression over the UN plan, not Israeli brutality or land confiscation, that caused the displacement of some Arabs.

The Palestinian 'Refugees' myth

Oddly enough, after more than 70 years, the displaced Arabs and their resulting generations are still being treated as refugees. Of all the world's refugees only the Palestinian 'refugees' have received this non-ending refugee status. The United Nations Relief and Works Agency for Palestine Refugees in the Near East (UNRWA) is only and solely for Palestinians. It's biggest donor, the USA, contributes more than $360 million of the agency's annual $1.25 billion budget. Historically, U.S. support to UNRWA has been 'untouchable' despite the agency's role in perpetually keeping Palestinians in social distress, providing welfare, education and health services while prohibiting resettlement efforts and continually building a culture of rejectionism of anything Israeli or Jewish. In doing so, they perpetuated the Palestinians' "refugee" status for decades and continue to do so into the foreseeable future.

---

4. Following the 1967 Six-Day war, Israel offered to negotiate the return of the West Bank and Gaza to the Arabs. At the Khartoum summit this proposal was rejected with "Three 'No's":
    ◆ No peace (with Israel)
    ◆ No recognition (of Israel)
    ◆ No negotiations (with Israel)
5. In 2000, Israeli Prime Minister Ehud Barak offered to create a Palestinian state, but Yasser Arafat rejected the deal and terror ensued.
6. In 2005, Israel unilaterally withdrew from the Gaza region, only to be rewarded with regular rocket attacks from the Hamas terrorists.

These are just a few examples of the many times that the British, the UN and Israel have offered land to the Arabs that could have been a Palestinian state. It was always rejected, because they would have to admit and accept the existence of a Jewish state.

Abba Eban Quotes

"The Arabs have never missed an opportunity...to miss an opportunity!"

"Time and again these governments have rejected proposals today - and longed for them tomorrow."

"Nobody does Israel any service by proclaiming its 'right to exist.' Israel's right to exist, like that of the United States, Saudi Arabia and 152 other states, is axiomatic and unreserved. Israel's legitimacy is not suspended in midair awaiting acknowledgement.... There is certainly no other state, big or small, young or old, that would consider mere recognition of its 'right to exist' a favor, or a negotiable concession."

ABOUT U.N.R.W.A and U.N.H.C.R

Members of the U.S. Congress are demanding to see a report that could change the entire Middle East political picture by answering one simple question: Has the attempt to produce a solution to the Israel-Palestinian problem been predicated on inflating the number of Palestinian refugees? And in addition, has the answer been hidden to fuel a multi-billion dollar political agenda, one which gives the Palestinians the upper-hand in peace negotiations?

The report was compiled under the Obama administration in 2015 but was immediately classified. According to a report in the Washington Free Beacon published in January 2018, that report is still being kept under wraps by the State Department. A Freedom of Information Act request, a lawsuit, and a letter from 51 members of Congress to Donald Trump have all tried to convince President Trump to declassify the report. U.S. lawmakers are demanding to see it due to the implications concerning the negotiations between Israel and the Palestinians.

The report is five pages long and its basis is simple. In normal parlance, a refugee is someone who has been forced to flee his or her country and cannot return because of persecution, war or violence. When Israel declared itself a nation in 1948, an estimated 700,000 Arabs fled the newly-formed state. Approximately 750,000-850,000 Jews either fled or were expelled from Arab countries at around the same time, although they were absorbed into Israel.

When the **United Nations Relief and Works Agency (UNRWA)** was established in 1949 to aid Palestinian refugees, the definition of 'refugee' was expanded to include all patrilineal descendants of any Arab that had lived in Israel for at least two years prior to being displaced by Israel's War of Independence in 1948. As a result of this open-ended inherited refugee status, the number of Palestinian refugees has  grown and UNRWA now claims there are an estimated 5.3 million registered patrilineal descendants of the original "Palestine refugees."

According to the report hidden away by the State Department which determines the number of Palestinian refugees who personally fled Israel as per the normal definition of the term 'refugee,' at around 20,000, not the invalid claim of 700,000.

It has also been criticized for prolonging the UNRWA's *raison d'etre* and swelling its pool of recipients. UNRWA is a big business. It is the United Nations' largest agency. It is the only UN agency dedicated to helping refugees from a specific region or conflict and its recipients receive more than twice the per capita aid of any other refugees.

The **UNHCR (United Nations High Commissioner for Refugees)** formed in 1950, is the main organization through which the world's other refugees are aided. The UNHCR has a specific mandate to aid its refugees to eliminate their refugee status by local integration in current country, resettlement in a third country or repatriation. By remaining under the auspices of the UNRWA, the conflict between the Palestinians and Israel is artificially prolonged.

The Palestinian Authority insists on the right of return for all 5.3 million of UNRWA Palestinians as a precondition to negotiations. This would be demographic suicide for Israel, a country of 6.5 million Jews.

To prevent this, Israeli Prime Minister Benjamin Netanyahu recently called for UNRWA to be abolished and for the Palestinian refugees to fall under the auspices of the UNHCR.

U.S. lawmakers are demanding to see the report because they have their own questions concerning UNRWA.

The U.S. has given an estimated $ 6 billion or more to UNRWA since 1950.

> *"Nothing is politically right,*
> *Which is morally wrong."*
> **Abraham Lincoln**

CHAPTER 14
The West Bank, Judea and Samaria and the 'Settlements'

Jews have lived in Judea and Samaria (West Bank) since ancient times.

The only time Jews were not allowed to live in this region was during Jordan's rule from 1948 to 1967. This prohibition was contrary to the Mandate for Palestine adopted by the League of Nations.

The mandate provided for the establishment of a Jewish National Home, and specifically encouraged "close settlement by Jews on the land," which included Judea and Samaria.

"I will bring forth descendants from Jacob, and from Judah those who will possess my mountains; my chosen people will inherit them, and there will my servants live." Isaiah 65:9

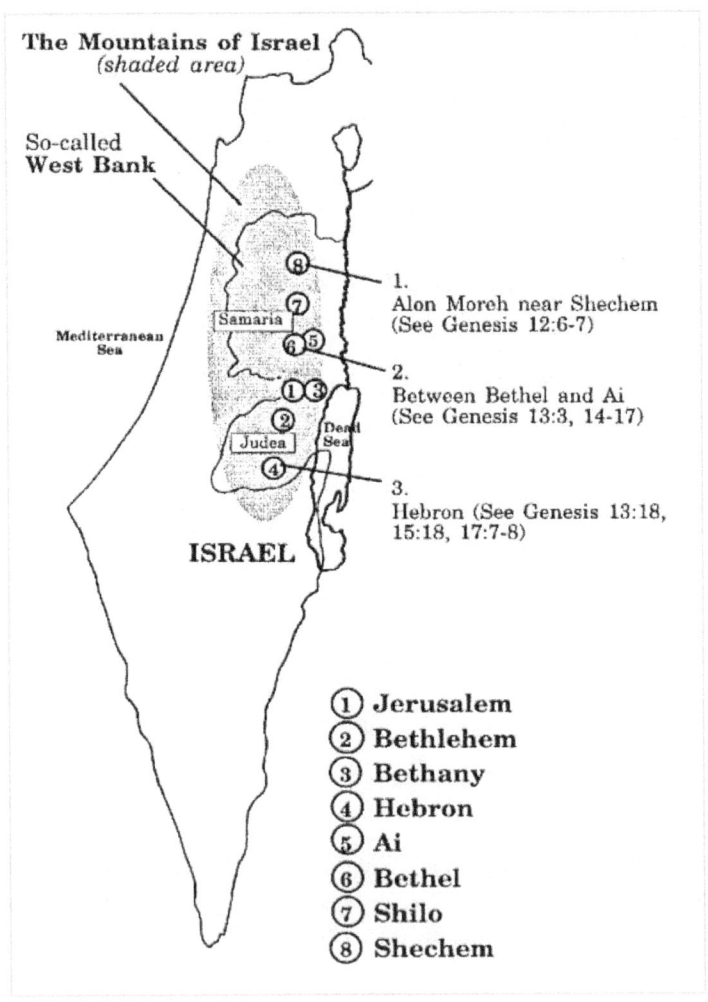

The Mountains of Israel
(shaded area)

So-called West Bank

Mediterranean Sea

Samaria

Judea

Dead Sea

ISRAEL

1.
Alon Moreh near Shechem
(See Genesis 12:6-7)

2.
Between Bethel and Ai
(See Genesis 13:3, 14-17)

3.
Hebron (See Genesis 13:18, 15:18, 17:7-8)

① Jerusalem
② Bethlehem
③ Bethany
④ Hebron
⑤ Ai
⑥ Bethel
⑦ Shilo
⑧ Shechem

Ezekiel 36 refers to the "Mountains of Israel" and this chapter specifically speaks of the future of those mountains. The "fake news" world continually refers to that land as the "occupied West Bank." Modern Israel calls them **Judea and Samaria,** hearkening back to the 1st and 2nd Temple Biblical periods.

Read Ezekiel 36 by substituting **"occupied west bank" for the "mountains of Israel"** and notice it sounds much more like the current cable news programs.

> *"'But you, "occupied West Bank", will produce branches and fruit for my people Israel, for they will soon come home. I am concerned for you and will look on you with favor; you will be plowed and sown, and I will cause many people to live on you—yes, all of Israel. The towns will be inhabited and the ruins rebuilt. I will increase the number of people and animals living on you, and they will be fruitful and become numerous. I will settle people on you ("occupied West Bank") as in the past and will make you prosper more than before. Then you will know that I am the LORD. I will cause people, my people Israel, to live on you. They will possess you, and you will be their inheritance; you will never again deprive them of their children." Ezekiel 36: 8-12*

It will not be a Palestinian State because the scripture clearly states in verse 8, *"'But you, **mountains of Israel,** will produce branches and fruit for my people Israel, for they will soon come home."* And verse 12: *"I will cause people, **my people Israel,** to live on you. They will possess you, and you will be their inheritance; you will never again deprive them of their children."*

When will we stop wasting time and money looking for some magic formula that will bring peace to the hearts of the Palestinian leadership and a state in the heart of Israel?
Former Israeli Prime Minister Arik Sharon stated the answer years ago as to where a Palestinian State should be established. He said, "They already have a state. It's called Jordan."

Maybe they should look at that as a possibility... because it isn't going to happen in Judea and Samaria.

Unless there is a permanent freeze on construction in Jewish settlements, Palestinian Chairman Mahmoud Abbas refuses to negotiate with Israel. Now during the Trump administration, Abbas finds a new reason with each presidential tweet to state his opposition to even meet with the Trump team.
Abbas will never live long enough to seriously sit down and negotiate with Israel or the United States. You can mark my words on that statement.

A few years ago, Prime Minister Benjamin Netanyahu responded to pressure from the international community to meet the demands of the Palestinian leadership. Even though construction was frozen for ten months, it was to no avail - the Palestinians still refused to negotiate with Israel. Also refusing to recognize Israel as a Jewish State, Abbas insists that the UN recognize the West Bank and Gaza as the Palestinian State. Each UN session is dominated by this demand.

In my opinion, it is impossible for any Palestinian leader to make any compromises with Israel. They have painted themselves into a corner and any negotiations, which naturally implies making compromises, would be signing their own death warrant.

To facilitate the Palestinians' avoidance to negotiate with Israel, our previous administration suggested that either the Quartet (UN, the European Union, Russia and the US) or former President Obama and John Kerry would pressure Israel into making "painful concessions".

The Obama administration demanded a return to the "1967 borders". However, there were never any actual borders, but only the 1949 "cease fire lines".

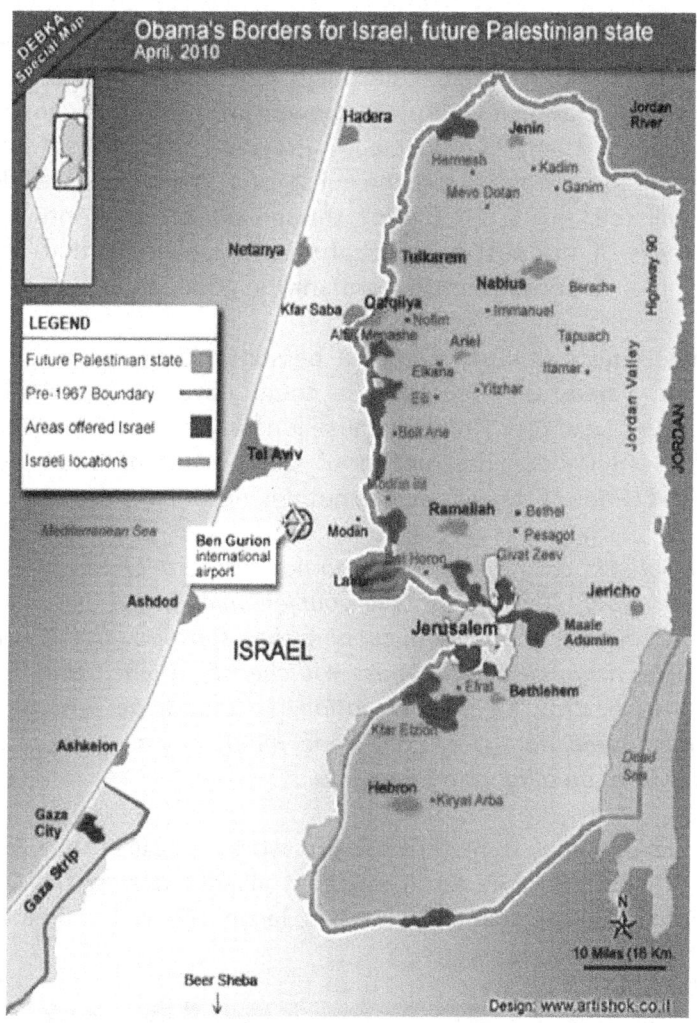

Obama's plan, 2010

Long ago, the US stated that the conflict would only be resolved when Israelis and Palestinians negotiate face-to-face. That International Law, known as UN Resolution 242, specifies that any land agreements must be negotiated with the Israeli government. That is exactly what Mahmoud Abbas consistently has refused to do. Israel is stymied because there is no Palestinian negotiating partner.

President Trump, who made his career by negotiating deals, calls a successful end to the Israeli-Palestinian conflict the "Ultimate Deal." However, he is also known to withdraw from deals and negotiations if he deems them "un-doable." Previous presidents found it impossible to walk away from the quest for a "Mideast Peace" deal. Time will tell, but I don't think this president will continue the foolishness of the past in negotiating with an entity that has no intention of compromising or negotiating in good faith.

Perhaps today's situation can best be summed up by reading the first five verses of Psalm 83. It could have been written for tomorrow's New York Times, because it describes world leaders who are focused on the destruction of God's Chosen People in His Promised Land. Certainly, there is nothing new under the sun.

> *"O God, do not remain silent; do not turn a deaf ear, do not stand aloof, O God. See how your enemies growl, how your foes rear their heads. With cunning they conspire against your people; they plot against those you cherish. "Come," they say, "let us destroy them as a nation, so that Israel's name is remembered no more." With one mind they plot together;* ***they form an alliance against you..."***

World leaders may think they are just working against the "Zionist" state, but in fact, they are forming an alliance against the God of Israel, the God of Abraham, Isaac and Jacob, the God and Father of Christ Jesus our Lord.

What do you think are the odds of them winning that battle?

In relationship to what we have read before, I have come to the following prediction (which are not prophecies, because I am not a prophet or the son of a prophet):

- The Palestinian Authority will never make peace with Israel and therefore, there will never be a Palestinian State established on the holy land of Israel.
- There will never be peace or a Palestinian state because the PA doesn't want either. This is the lesson of the past 70 years. Both Abbas and his predecessor, PLO leader Arafat, rejected peace and statehood multiple times and opted instead to expand their terrorist and political war against Israel.

Why did they do that?

Because they are interested in two things: personal enrichment – achieved by stealing donor funds and emptying the pockets of their own people; and secondly, their goal is to progressively weaken and finally to destroy Israel by any means they can devise. It is as simple and bald-faced as that! These diabolical maniacal creatures absolutely cannot make peace because that would be absolutely opposed to all they have lived and believed in during the past seven decades. Even if they wanted to change, this would be an impossible task because of the success they had at political and terroristic warfare.

Isaiah 62:1 says, _"For Zion's sake I will not keep silent, and for Jerusalem's sake I will not keep quiet."_

Our nation's present and future well-being is linked to our attitude towards Israel, which actually is our attitude toward God. The Jewish people must be important to you, because our well-being as individuals is also linked to how we stand on God's Word, as is the future of our nation.

From the rise and fall of the British Empire, we learn what happens to a nation that chooses not to heed Genesis 12:3. They became a curse instead of a blessing to the apple of God's eye. (Zechariah 2:8)

CHAPTER 15
What Can YOU Do?

1. **Pray.**
   The Bible commands us to pray for the peace of Jerusalem -
   > *"Pray for the peace of Jerusalem.*
   > *May they prosper who love you." Psalm 122:6*

2. **Be a watchman on the walls of Jerusalem.**
   > *"On your walls, O Jerusalem, I have appointed watchmen;*
   > *All day and all night they will never keep silent;*
   > *You who remind the LORD, take no rest for yourselves;*
   > *And give Him no rest until He establishes*
   > *And makes Jerusalem a praise in the earth." Isaiah 62:6*

3. **We are to speak out for Zion's sake.**
   > *"For Zion's sake I will not keep silent,*
   > *And for Jerusalem's sake I will not keep quiet." Isaiah 62:1*

Why should we speak up?

> *"If you say, "But we knew nothing about this," does not He who weighs the heart perceive it? Does not He who guards your life know it? Will He not repay everyone according to what they have done?" Proverbs 24:12*

> *"For if you remain silent at this time, relief and deliverance for the Jews will arise from another place..." Esther 4:14*

4. **Intercede for Israel.**
   > *"And I sought for a man among them, that should make up the hedge, and stand in the gap before me for the land..."*
   > *Ezekiel 22:30*

5. **Learn from History.**
"Those who cannot remember the past are condemned to repeat it"

6. **Learn the truth and facts.**
"My people are destroyed from lack of knowledge."
Hosea ben Beeri 650 BC

Those who don't, will end up **SAD**
⇒ **S**urrendered
⇒ **A**pathetic
⇒ **D**enial

Ignorance means: lacking knowledge about a particular subject.

7. **Choose your leaders wisely.**
Wall Street Journal quoted Billy Graham in their Oct 18, 2012 edition:

"As I approach my 94th birthday, I realize this election could be my last. I believe it is vitally important that we cast our ballots for candidates who base their decisions on Biblical principles and support the nation of Israel. I urge you to vote for those who protect the sanctity of life and support the Biblical definition of marriage between a man and a woman. Vote for Biblical values this November 6, and pray with me that America will remain one nation under God."

There is an ideological battle going on among Christians:

a. Should Christians involve themselves in the world by participating in politics, pursue advanced degrees in education, medicine, science and law, produce films, seek careers in journalism, and develop non-governmental programs for long-term social reform based on a well-thought -out Biblical worldview?

b. Should Christians spend their lives in so-called full-time Christian service and reject the world? A well-known pastor argues for a narrowly focused gospel agenda: "We are interested in people becoming saved. That is our only agenda ... It is the only thing that we are in the world to do."

If we are going to see our nation transformed, it has to be done from the inside out, that's our agenda.

But how? Can we do it from afar, cloistered behind the walls of the sanctuary?
Could the Samaritan who helped the man who "fell among robbers" (Luke 10:30–37) have demonstrated compassion by only preaching the gospel?
At the conclusion of the story, Jesus told His audience to "go and do likewise" (10:37).

> *"We must always take sides.*
> *Neutrality helps the oppressor, never the victim.*
> *Silence encourages the tormentor,*
> *never the tormented."*
> **Elie Wiesel**

There is no neutrality.

I can assure Christians everywhere that if we are not applying our faith, those opposed to our faith will be applying theirs.

If governmental policies are hurting the poor by making them dependent on the State, how can Christians ignore the political process that reinforces multi-generational poverty in the name of "social justice"?

The Bible has a great deal to say about the oppression of the poor by individuals and governments (1 Kings 21:1–16; Eccl. 5:8; Isa. 3:14; 10:2; Ezek. 22:29; Amos 4:1; Zech. 7:10).

Saying "it's the government's job" to deal with poverty, jobs, and housing is akin to saying, "go in peace, be warmed and be filled" (James 2:16). Today's poor are more oppressed by governments than by individuals.

A Good-Samaritan Faith or a GENESIS 12:3 Church requires Christians becoming involved in politics in order to halt the oppression of the poor by policies that make people dependent upon the State.

This doesn't mean that we should stop preaching Gospel, but it does mean that there are other duties for Christians to perform.

The Christian faith and Christians are under attack.

The day may come, because of our self-imposed silence, that we will be forced into silence as a matter of law.

> *"There may be times when we are*
> *powerless to prevent injustice,*
> *but there must never be a time*
> *when we fail to protest."*
> **Elie Wiesel**

Then what will we do?

By What Standards are Nations Judged by God?

Nations have been, they are, and they will be judged by how they treat Israel and the Jewish people.

"I tremble for my country when I recall that God is just, and that His justice will not sleep forever."

Thomas Jefferson

"You have been weighed on the scales and found wanting."
Daniel 5:27

"The day of the LORD is near for all nations. As you have done, it will be done to you; your deeds will return upon your own head." Obadiah 1:15

CHURCHILL QUOTES

"You can always count on Americans to do the right thing – after they've tried everything else."

"Courage is the first of human qualities because it is the quality which guarantees all others."

The United States:

The Key to Israel's Security

Or is it the other way around?

Israel:

The Key to the Security

of the United States

Zion's Watchmen

Our ministry, "Zion's Watchmen", is based on Isaiah 62:1

"For Zion's sake I will not keep silent,
and for Jerusalem's sake
I will not keep quiet."

Traditionally, watchmen have stood on the ramparts of their city, peering out at the landscape.
The moment they saw danger coming, they alerted the populace and the militia.
That is one of the missions we as Zion's Watchmen have for our own nation and especially as it relates to Israel.
We are calling out to all who listen and who seriously observe what Scripture says. We also

remind them of what happened to other empires.
Nations truly are judged by God when they violate His principles as they relate to Zion.

- ♦ We want you to be a watchman on the wall.
- ♦ We want you to stand up and say what the Word of God says and to warn our elected leaders: "Don't step over those lines. Stop this deadly game of pushing for a Palestinian State that would divide the land."
- ♦ We are to speak out. That has been the problem for Christians around the world in the last 20, 30, 40, and 50 years.

My mother always told me: "Johnny, don't talk about religion and don't talk about politics with people."

"Sorry, mom! That's all I talk about, because they are intertwined."

If your beliefs from Scripture don't affect your politics, you are missing the boat. What makes you think they can be separated? They are inevitably linked together.

We will continue to do our very best to speak to Power, to the White House, to Congress, to city and county governments, to school boards, etc. I believe that God has people who are waiting to hear and others who are already listening and just need us to wake them up.

♦ We are to speak out for Zion's sake. Isaiah 62:1 says, *"For Zion's sake I will not keep silent, and for Jerusalem's sake I will not keep quiet."*

Our nation's present and future well-being is linked to our attitude towards Israel which actually is our attitude toward God.

The Jewish people must be important to you! Our wellbeing as individuals is also linked to how we stand on God's word, as is the future of our nation.

America stands with Israel because her cause is our cause, her values are our values, and her fight is our fight.
– Vice President Mike Pence

Zion's Watchmen TOURS

Come and visit the Land that God calls, "My Land"!

Because of the total immersion in the land and the culture where the Bible was written, these tours have often been described as "life changing". Be assured: this trip will definitely change the way that you read and understand your Bible. While visiting the authentic places, John Somerville, David Simmons and other Israeli experts will teach about the Biblical culture. This Bible-based tour will also equip you to better understand the geo-political current (and future) events as you meet the people and hear from some world-renowned experts that visit us.

> **WARNING:** Visiting Israel can be life-changing and dangerous to all your future vacation plans (Cancun will lose its luster). It is more than likely that your heart will be touched, and you fall in love with the Land and the People that God calls, "My Land" and "My Chosen people."

Zion's Watchmen Tours are led and organized by John Somerville and his Ministry partner, David Simmons.

"Zion's Watchmen's" Co-Director and Vice President David Simmons has been a minister for over 40 years. He also served as the National Cowboy Church Coordinator for CUFI.

John and David travel extensively to countries that are affected by the events in the Middle East.

Tour contact information:

⇒ Telephone: +1 559-877-2882.
  Mobile (559) 760-5410

⇒ Email: israel4somerville@gmail.com

⇒ Website: israelsomerville.com

⇒ Facebook: Zion's Watchmen/Tour Israel

Israel Network TV

You can watch John Somerville's teaching on this subject (and many others) by visiting the website of Israel TV Network Channel.
Website: https://israeltvnetwork.tv

The network offers a variety of television programs dedicated to sharing the teachings of the Bible, love for the Jewish People, and support for the land of Israel. The programs come from both Jewish and Christian teachers dedicated to the authentic message of the Bible.

John's teachings are part of a series called "The White House and Israel". He also speaks about the "Roots of the Holocaust and anti-semitism", the "Muddled Middle East" and this book's title:
The Rise and Fall of the British Empire.

SAVE A CHILD'S HEART (SACH)

Zion's Watchmen sponsors the SACH organization. SACH patients are brought to Israel to be treated at the Wolfson Medical Center in Holon.

Approximately 50% of the children are from the Palestinian Authority, Jordan, Iraq and Morocco; more than 30% are from Africa; and the remaining are from Asia, Eastern Europe and the Americas.

To date, SACH has treated more than 2,900 children suffering from congenital and rheumatic heart disease, aged 0 to 18 years of age from 43 countries.

For more info, please visit website: www.saveachildsheart.org

We put our heart into saving a child's life

EZRA INTERNATIONAL

Zion's Watchmen is affiliated with Ezra International, an organization based on Isaiah 11:12,

"And He will lift up a standard for the nations and assemble the banished ones of Israel, and will gather the dispersed of Judah from the four corners of the earth."

EZRA's goal is the Rescue, Return and Restoration of poor Jewish People to Israel.

Ezra International is a Christian non-profit organization that helps the poorest of the poor Jewish people make Aliyah (emigrate to Israel). The return of Jewish people to Israel today is a fulfillment of God's Promise made centuries ago. For 2,000 years, it seemed impossible. But now it's happening and scripture also promised that you can be a part of it! Read More.

Ezra's Logo: God is at the center of it all and He is reaching out to the four corners of the earth. He is re-gathering His people back to Israel and you can help provide a light to show the way home.

For more info, please visit website: www. ezrainternational.org

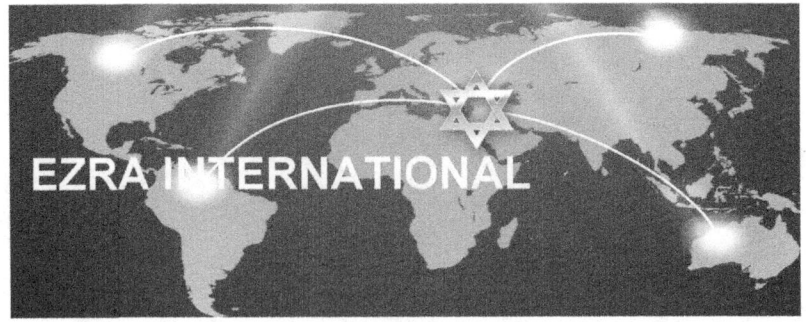

ABOUT JOHN AND MARY SOMERVILLE

Col. John Somerville USMC (ret.) is Director of "Zion's Watchmen",
a non-profit ministry registered in Texas, USA.

A graduate of both the Naval and Army War Colleges, John earned a
Ph.D. from Ohio State University. During his military active duty, he
served in many countries around the world.

John's interest in the Middle East has taken him into the region more
than 70 times over the past 40 years. During this time, he has led
many tour groups to Israel, coached Israeli youth baseball camps and
volunteered on numerous archaeological digs.

Meanwhile, Mary was fighting the battles of the home front while
raising their own fire-team of six little warriors.

Through lectures, TV broadcasts and other media, John diligently
works to build understanding and support for Israel. By utilizing
supporters, John and Mary and their partners hope to impact
American foreign policy by communicating a pro-Israel perspective to
our elected officials.

Zion's Watchmen is committed to the Biblical mandate to bless,
speak out and stand with Israel and the Jewish people.

John and Mary (married for 50+ years), make their home on a ranch
in North Fork, California, USA.

SELECTED BIBLIOGRAPHY

The Gifts of the Jews
Cahill, Thomas
Doubleday (New York, 1998)

The Trials of Zion
Dershowitz, Alan M.
Grand Central Pub. (New York, 2010)

War in the Holy Land from Megiddo to the West Bank
Duncan, Andrew and Opatowski, Michel
Sutton Publishing (Hong Kong, 1998)

Old Testament Bible History
Edersheim, Alfred

Empire, The Rise and Demise of the British World Order And the Lessons for Global Power
Ferguson, Niall
Penguin Books (England, 2002)

Empire by Treaty
Fitzsimons, M.A.
University of Notre Dame Press
(Notre Dame IN, 1964)

Nazi Germany and the Jews 1933-1945
Friedlander, Saul
Haerper Perennial (New York, 2009)

From the Ends of the Earth: The Jews in the Twentieth Century
Gilbert, Martin
Polo Pub. (London, 1997)

The Fight for Jerusalem
Gold, Dore
Regnery Publishing, Inc. Washington, DC, 2007)

The Battle for Jerusalem
Gur, Mordechai
Popular Library (Brooklyn, N.Y., 1973)

Like Dreamers
Halevi, Yossi Klein
Harper Collins (New York, 2013)

Mein Kampf
Hitler, Adolf Translated by Ralph Manheim
Houghton Mifflin Co. (New York, 1971)

Israel God's Key
Josephson, Elmer A.
Bible Light Pub. (Hillsboro, Kansas, 1974)

Jewish Roots
Juster, Dan
Destiny Image (Shippensburg, PA 1995)

The Jewish Book of Why
Kolatch, Alfred J.
Penguin Group (New York, 2003)

What is a Jew?
Kertzer, Rabbi Morris
Macmillan Pub. (New York, 1960)

A Middle East Mosaic - Fragments of Life, letters and history
Lewis, Bernard
Random House (New York, 2000)

1938 Hitler's Gamble
Macdonogh, Giles
Constable & Robinson Ltd (EU, 2009)

Paris 1919
MacMillan, Margaret
Random House (New York, 2003)

Churchill's Promised Land-Zroman and Statecraft
Makovsky, Michael
Yale University Press (New Haven, 2007)

The Rothschilds
Morton, Frederic
Crest Book (New York, 1961)

1948 – The First Arab – Israeli War
Morris, Benny
Yale University Press (New Haven, 2008)

The Climax of an Empire
Morris, James
Harcourt Brace Jovanovich (New York, 1968)

The Genesis Record
Morris, Henry M
Baker Book House (Grand Rapids, Mich. 1976)

Hamas Jihad
Ne'eman, Yisrael
White Hart Pub (USA 2016)

Ally, My Journey across the American-Israeli Divide
Oren, Michael B.
Random House (New York, 2015)

The Paradise of God
Ollison, Larry
Harrison House Pub. (Tulsa, Oklahoma, 2014)

Why the Jews?
Prager, Dennis and Telushkin, Joseph   Simon and Schuster (New York, 2003)

The Stones Cry Out
Price, Randall
Harvest House (Eugene, 1977)

A Safe Haven
Radosh, Allis and Radosh, Ronald
Harper Collins (New York, 2009)

One Palestine Complete, Jews and Arabs under the British Mandate
Segev, Tom
Henry Holt & Company (New York, 1999)

Start-Up Nation
Senor, Dan and Singer, Saul
Hatchette Book Group (New York, 2009)

British Lives in Palestine 1918 - 1948
Sherman, A.J.
Thames and Hudson (New York, 1997)

Why Israel Matters to You
Spero, Aryeh
Evergreen Press (Mobile, 2015)

The New Strong's Complete Dictionary of Bible Words
Strong, James
Thomas Nelson Pub. (Nashville, Tenn., 1996)

Bible and Sword
Tuchman, Barbara W.
Ballantine Books (New York, 1984)

The Innocents Abroad
Twain, Mark
Readers Digest Assoc. (Pleasantville, N.Y., 1990)

Twilight
Wiesel, Elie
Summit Books (New York, 1987)

Night
Wiesel, Elie
Holt, Rinehart and Winston (Austin, Texas, 1960)

Jerusalem as Jesus Knew it - Archaeology as Evidence
Wilkinson, John
Thames and Hudson (Yugoslavia, 1988)

And I will make of thee a great nation, and I will bless thee, and make thy name great; and thou shalt be a blessing: And I will bless them that bless thee, and curse him that curseth thee: and in thee shall all families of the earth be blessed.
Genesis 12:2-3

Made in the USA
Monee, IL
07 July 2026

56551411R00069